Call to Discipleship

A Literary Study of Mark's Gospel

GOOD NEWS STUDIES

Volume 1

Call to Discipleship

A Literary Study of Mark's Gospel

by

Augustine Stock, OSB

Michael Glazier, Inc.
Wilmington, Delaware

First published in 1982 by Michael Glazier, Inc.
1723 Delaware Avenue, Wilmington, Delaware 19806
and Veritas Publications, 7/8 Lower Abbey St., Dublin, Ireland

Library of Congress Catalog Card Number: 82-81396
International Standard Book Number:
  Good News Studies: 0-89453-290-1
  CALL TO DISCIPLESHIP: 0-89453-273-1

Printed in the United States of America

CONTENTS

INTRODUCTION

MARK HAD LONG BEEN the neglected gospel. And even when, in this century, it had become a focus of interest, its writer did not fare too well. Form-criticism seemed to have shown Mark up as a clumsy compiler. Redaction critics were able to discern some sort of framework; Mark was rehabilitated after a fashion. But, too often, form and redaction criticism had got in the way of an overall view of the gospel. Recently — and notably in the United States — there has been a happy development: Mark is seriously regarded as an *author* and his gospel a literary work. Biblical literary criticism — building on the worthwhile insights of form and redaction criticism — is contributing to a better understanding of the gospel.

Once we have accepted that a gospel is a book and an evangelist an author, remarkable things begin to happen — remarkable only because we have faced the obvious. We had tended to regard a gospel as a string of passages. We had been mezmerized by the analysis of the form-critics and had grown accustomed to a synoptic study: constantly comparing two or more parallel passages. Once the gospel is taken as a literary whole it appears in a refreshingly new light.

Viewed this way, the second gospel takes on further depth and meaning. Mark is recognized as a writer who had written purposefully and planned his writing with care. He had, of course, made extensive use of traditional material because he wrote for a community with a firm christian tradition. But he knew what he was about and he exploited his sources with notable freedom and with skill. He has written our gospel: a literary work and a document of sterling theological worth. The traditional *kata Marcon* ("according to Mark") should be given its full weight. The commonsense approach is to look at the gospel as a whole.

Augustine Stock, O.S.B., has done just that. He has found it to be a dramatic work bearing traces of the influence of contemporary Greek dramatic art — corresponding indeed to the basic pattern of Greek drama. He has sought enlightenment in both ancient Greek and modern western literary theory. His application of the theory to the work of Mark is judicious and revealing. Time and again he is able to shed new light on areas of the gospel and discern fresh meaning. His chosen road of literary criticism is surely a right way to a better understanding of Mark. His is an important and rewarding study. He leads the reader into an appreciation of this deceptively simple gospel, to a feeling for its dramatic quality — above all, to an awareness of its challenge. More than ever will one realise that this voice out of the past carries a peremptory message to the present.

Wilfrid Harrington, O.P.

CHAPTER 1
LITERARY CRITICS AND
BIBLE CRITICS

IN 1978 VETERAN BRITISH ACTOR Alec McCowen had memorized Mark's gospel and was reciting it on stage in London and New York to rave notices. For some time McCowen had felt that the gospels had been neglected by the stage and media and that they had come to carry a negative meaning. He resolved to bring a gospel to the stage and to emphasize the "good news" aspect as strongly as possible. After some experimentation he discovered that Mark worked best for the purpose he had in mind. He is reported to have said later: "Mark was the greatest script I ever found."[1]

Some biblical scholars found McCowen's emphasis on the "good news" aspect, and especially his use of the long ending, unsatisfactory. In an article entitled "*St. Mark* on Stage: Laughing all the Way to the Cross," John Koenig writes that McCowen's rendition failed "as a theologically reponsible interpretation."[2] Actually Mark depicts Jesus as a man increasingly isolated, misunderstood, and rejected, even by his closest associates.

[1] *Time Magazine*, March 10, 1980, p. 65.
[2] *Theology Today*, 36(1979), 84-8.

Interpretative defects aside, McCowen had a real accomplishment to his credit. He had perceived that Mark's gospel is a unified literary work and he had brought it to the stage. McCowen's reciting Mark's gospel on the stage with such resounding success is a bit of evidence about that gospel that cannot be ignored. And (apparently unbeknownst to McCowen) he carried this off at a time when some biblical scholars had begun to approach biblical writings in just this way, as integrated wholes, as totalities proceeding from a single mind. And a few were even advancing the theory that Mark's gospel had been written to be presented just as McCowen was doing.

Biblical Literary Criticism

This new movement in Bible interpretation is Biblical Literary Criticism (also called Rhetorical or Composition Criticism). It has grown out of and is a response to what preceded it, form criticism and redaction criticism.

The purpose of form criticism was to get behind the sources of the gospels and to describe what was happening as the tradition about Jesus was handed on orally from person to person and from community to community. Form criticism was especially concerned with the modifications which the life and thought of the Church introduced into the tradition, and form critics were convinced that they had worked out criteria for distinguishing those strata in the gospels which reflect the concerns of the Church from the stratum that might be thought to go back to the historical Jesus. They were also convinced that the Church's vital life had contributed formal characteristics to the tradition, making it possible to classify much of the material in the gospels according to literary form. Form criticism concerned itself largely with investigating the individual units, stories and sayings, in the gospels.

Redaction criticism grew out of form criticism but represents a step toward reintegration. The redaction critic investigates how smaller units from the oral and written sources were put together to form larger complexes and he is especially interested in the formation of the gospels as finished products. "Its goals are to understand why the items from the tradition were modified and connected as they were, to identify the theological motifs that were at work in composing a finished Gospel, and to elucidate the theological point of view which is expressed in and through the composition."[3]

The redaction critic "attaches the most value to what the author revised in his source. Generally that which the author added or changed is considered more important than what he adopts. One can ask oneself what the reason for this is. One will receive nowhere an explicit answer, but one can surmise that this sort of active operations on a given text are assumed to require more attention from the author than the more passive acceptance."[4]

While they are similar in some aspects, today biblical literary criticism and redaction criticism are seen to be clearly distinct. Redaction criticism is literary in its intention to observe and analyze how the final author of a gospel (or other document) shaped and modified his source materials (tradition) and put them together. But it still wants to separate tradition from redaction (the author's contribution), and general literary critics regard this procedure with suspicion.

Windows and Mirrors

Literary critics point out that the shift of analytical focus from the literary whole to the preliterary parts has had the effect of dissolving the whole. By basing their

[3]Dan O. Via, Foreword to Norman Perrin, *What is Redaction Criticism?* (Philadelphia: Fortress Press, 1969), p. vi.

[4]B. Van Iersel and A. Linmans, "'The storm on the Lake' Mk iv 35-41 and Mt viii 18-27 in the light of Form Criticism, 'Redaktionsgeschichte' and Structural Analysis," *Supplement to Novum Testamentum* 48, *Miscellanea Neotestamentica*, Vol. 2, p. 48.

method on the distinction between redaction and tradition, redaction critics are forced to look *through* the text by focusing on the relations between it and its sources. As a consequence they cannot look *at* the text in order to see how the units in its linear sequence are related to one another to form the whole. Thus, applying this to Mark, Robert C. Tannehill writes: "Preoccupation with the pre-Gospel units of tradition and with the editorial modification of those units obscured the fact that Mark is a continuous narrative presenting a meaningful development to a climax and that each episode should be understood in light of its relation to the story as a whole."[5]

Literary criticism moves away from bondage to the distinction between tradition and redaction as the only gateway to Markan theology. It regards Mark in its final form as the product of one creative mind. Questions of tradition and redaction are comparatively unimportant: what matters is the function of the text concerned in the gospel as a whole.

If such is the attitude of literary critics toward the restrained distinctions of redaction critics, one can foresee what their attitude toward form critics will be. For them form critics are "disintegrators." They had dealt with such people in their own field. During the nineteenth century and the first decades of the twentieth, it was fashionable among literary critics to engage in "disintegration." Looking at the available Shakespearean texts, for example, critics would suggest, for any of a number of plausible reasons, that certain passages did not represent what Shakespeare himself had written. Their aim was to rediscover the real Shakespeare by eliminating from the corpus whatever they found to be aesthetically or morally unacceptable to their best understanding of Shakespeare.

The Disintegrators

The disintegrators hypothesized lost earlier texts (of whose mere existence there is often no evidence) in order

[5]*Interpretation*, 34(1980), 148.

to account for elements in Shakespeare's canon that they found objectionable. They attempted to ascribe these variously according to systems that they claimed were scientific and inexorable. General literary critics did not find the systems to be either scientific or inexorable. They further objected that the disintegrators were violating the most basic of all critical principles: that the critic is not free to alter, or deny, or ignore the text in order to suit his own presuppositions or needs or desires. The detailed and impressive analyses of the disintegrators, critics now say, moved from equivocal uses of evidence to subjective conclusions. The efforts of the form critics involve essentially the same *modus operandi*: to separate strata belonging to different dates within the gospels, so as to disclose the process of redaction or to identify the authentic earliest stratum.

Biblical Literary Criticism arose from criticism which literary critics leveled against Bible critics. In her *Business of Criticism* (1959)[6] Dame Helen Gardner cited a strong reaction against the study of even extant and known sources, much more against the discussion of hypothetical ones. Vigorous articles by Roland M. Frye, Professor of English at the University of Pennsylvania, have been printed and reprinted. Frye questions the practicability of separating what Jesus actually said from redactional additions ascribed to him, since there is no literary-historical methodology that can perform this separation with any assurance.[7] Northrop Frye, University of Toronto, argues that "the tremendous cultural influence of the Bible is inexplicable by any criticism of it which stops where it begins to look like something with the literary form of a specialist's stamp collection."[8]

The same points are now being made by some biblical scholars who have come alive to the objections of historians

[6](Oxford: Clarendon Press, 1959), p. 98.

[7]"Literary Criticism and Gospel Criticism," *Theology Today*, 36(1979), 217.

[8]*Anatomy of Criticism*, (Princeton: Princeton University Press, 1957), p. 315.

and literary critics. They recognize that the practice of New Testament exegesis often leads historians to ask whether it really has anything at all to do with historico-critical method. "Not only do form criticism and redaction criticism presuppose irreconcilably different roles for the individual and the community in the creation of the New Testament writings. Even those scholars using the same disciple often come to diametrically opposed conclusions because they start with different unverifiable assumptions concerning the historical situation out of which the books were written."[9] They take as their starting point a hypothetical reconstruction of earliest Christianity, rather than the texts which have actually come down to us. Historical criticism has continued to hold sway in biblical studies long after it has ceased to be the dominant mode of literary criticism.

To be sure, their approach also has its drawbacks and limitations. The believer who reads too exclusively in this type of interpretation is apt to sense that the historical core, the central image of Jesus' life and death, seem to be disappearing.

A reasonable collaboration between historical and literary critics seems to be called for. At the conclusion of a survey of works by scholars trained in the philology of biblical and cognate languages and in the history and archaeology of the biblical regions and periods, J. D. Crossan affirms that it is clear "that such training has not produced experts sensitive to biblical literature precisely as literature but it is not at all clear to me that such sensitivity can be developed *without* this basic training. In other words, I would suggest that, despite or because of certain very interesting experiments...*sustained* excellence in the literary structuralism of biblical texts will necessitate linguistic and historical competencies as well as literary and structural sophistication."[10]

[9]Schuyler Brown, S.J., "Biblical Philology, Linguistics and the Problem of Method," *Heythrop Journal*, 20(1979), 297.

[10]"Waking the Bible, Biblical Hermeneutic and Literary Imagination,"*Interpretation*, 23(1978), 281-282.

At the present time (early 1980's) the future of Biblical Literary Criticism seems promising. The editorial of the April, 1980, number of *Interpretation* notes that: "The dominance of historical-critical exegesis seems to be on the wane. A perceptible wariness and weariness at the constantly pressing questions about the history of the text's formation and about the history to which the text refers or assumes, as though, in combination they were *the* interpretative question, has set in. Other candidates for the office of presiding over the approach to biblical texts are campaigning vigorously."[11]

In April, 1981, J. D. Kingsbury contributed an article entitled "The 'Divine Man' as the Key to Mark's Christology—the End of an Era?" Among the problem areas occupying his attention are the scholarly probe of the pre-Markan tradition, and the inclination to find the interpretative key to Mark's Christology outside his gospel. One of his conclusions is that "in principle any thesis which requires that the interpretative key to Mark's Christology be found outside his Gospel is suspect from the outset."[12] As he sees it the interpreter's task "is not to read the Gospel in terms of a reconstruction of the pre-Markan tradition or of the alleged heresy of Mark's church, but to follow the contours of Mark's story."[13]

[11]34(1980), 182.
[12]*Interpretation*, 35(1981), 251.
[13]*Ibid.*, 252.

CHAPTER 2
THE ORIGINS OF DRAMA

OUR GENERATION is discovering that the Bible, whatever else it may be, is certainly literature, and demands that we exercise upon it the methods and skills appropriate to the discussion of such problems. This discovery has been especially difficult for moderns to make in the case of Mark's gospel, since it has come to be regarded as particularly "unliterary."

But whether we find Mark "unliterary" or not will depend largely on what our expectations were; what kind of literature we were expecting? There are a number of literary genres into which Mark is seen to fit according to one critic or another. Helen Gardner thinks Mark is writing "something nearer a poem than a treatise."[1] Professor Roland M. Frye thinks that Mark's gospel fits into the category of *dramatic history*, of which Shakespeare was a masterful practitioner.

In the short two-hour traffic of his drama Shakespeare could not present events or personages "in their huge and proper life." Selection, condensation, here is even more necessary than it is elsewhere. What is presented about historical characters and events should be representative of the whole, but not exhaustive. Chronology must often

---

[1] *Business*, 102-03.

be telescoped. "What is shown represents a vastly larger canvas of life which cannot be shown."[2]

Getting on with the Story

And what qualities would Mark have if he were following the dramatic form even more closely? Even greater succinctness. Quite a number of eminent novelists have tried their hand at playwriting, but very few have succeeded. The techniques are so different that to have learned how to write a novel is of no help when it comes to writing a play. The novelist has all the time he wants to develop his theme; he can describe his characters as minutely as he chooses and make their behavior plain to the reader by relating their motives. He can gradually work up to a climax; he does not have to show action, but only to write about.

But a play depends on action. "The power of attention that an audience has is very limited, and it must be held by a constant succession of incidents; something fresh must be doing all the time; the theme must be presented at once and its development must follow a definite line, without digression into irrelevant bypaths."[3] A play cannot afford loose ends; therefore the playwright who turns to the novel is at an advantage. He has learned to stick to his point and get on with his story; he has learned to make his characters display themselves by their words and actions without the help of description.

By Mark's time the dramatic, rhetorical, and historical forms were well blended and Mark's work flows out of this situation.[4] In view of the clash between Judaism and Hellenism at the time of the Maccabeean revolt, many

[2]"A Literary Perspective for the Criticism of the Gospels." In *Jesus and Man's Hope*, Vol. 2, (Pittsburgh: Pittsburgh Theological Seminary, 1971), p. 209.

[3]W. Somerset Maugham, Introduction to *Tom Jones*, (Philadelphia: Winston, 1948), p. xix.

[4]Benoit Standaert, O.S.B., *L'Evangile selon Marc: Composition et Genre Litteraire*, (Brugge: Sint Andreisabdij, 1978).

would react negatively to the suggestion that there should be such a close contact between Hellenism and biblical writings. But it is quite clear today that before and after the Maccabeean revolt, Judaism was fairly saturated with Hellenistic ideas and culture. The idea that there was a huge gap between Palestinian Judaism and Hellenistic Judaism was an unfortunate result of F. C. Baur's attempt to apply Hegelian dialectic to the emergence of Christianity. The theory demanded it, so that is the way it had to be, but history and archaeology have shown that that is not the way it is.

Jerusalem and Athens

Historians who are at home in both Hellenistic and Jewish culture have shown that certain usages of the rabbis—the dialectic method, the explication of ancient texts, the expansion of ancient stories, the system of "difficulties and solutions," the relationship between teacher and disciple—were parallel to Greek usages. Since these usages were introduced after the spread of Hellenism, they might actually have been inspired by Greek practice. Jewish love of learning may owe much to the same influence.

And how widespread was the knowledge of Greek drama? For those who wrote in Greek there can be no question. Professor Moses Hadas has written that "it may be stated categorically that every bit of Greek writing we have (aside from such things as tax receipts and bills of sale), whatever the origins of the writer, shows knowledge of Greek tragedy. Every work in the Apocrypha and Pseudepigrapha of the Old Testament has expressions from or allusions to tragedy which the reader was obviously expected to recognize."[5]

Significant for the connection between classical drama and biblical writings is the fact that drama was originally of a religious nature. But at this point it is useful to interject a caveat that C. S. Lewis makes regarding the Hebrew

[5]*Hellenistic Culture, Form and Diffusion*, (Morningside Heights, N.Y.: Columbia University Press, 1959), p. 130.

psalmists, viz., that they did "not in fact distinguish between the love of God in what we might (rather dangerously) call 'a spiritual sense' and their enjoyment of the festivals in the Temple."[6]

Harm has been done in the past by the cliché that classical Greek dramas were part of a religious ritual. In a sense this is true, "but it was a ritual of a religion not at all like Christianity, though less unlike the Catholicism of Southern Europe or the Orthodox religion of the Greeks than it is unlike the Protestantism of Northern Europe. The religious element did not mean that the element of enjoyment was not important."[7]

A student of the Old Testament soon becomes acquainted with the nature or fertility gods of the Fertile Crescent, the Baals and the Ashtarts whom the prophets denounced with such vehemence. There, men viewed the fruitfulness of the soil in a religious way. The ground, it was said, is the sphere of divine power. The Baal of a region is the "lord" or "owner" of the ground; its fertility is dependent upon sexual relations between him and his consort. Furthermore, man was not a mere spectator of the sacred marriage which resurrected new life after the barrenness of winter. By ritually enacting the drama of Baal it was possible to assist— through magical power—the fertility powers to reach their consummation, and thereby to insure the welfare and prosperity of the land. The nature gods were, therefore, dying and rising gods; C. S. Lewis calls them "corn kings." Similar deities and rituals were found also in the Greek world, but here something new and significant grew out of the rituals of these cults—drama, both tragedy and comedy.

Dionysus

In the Greek world the fertility cult got attached especially to Dionysus (Bacchus). Originally a minor figure

---

[6]*Reflections on the Psalms*, (New York: Harcourt, Brace & World, 1958), p. 46.

[7]Hugh Lloyd-Jones, "The Greeks: a failure to face up to tragedy," *Times Literary Supplement*, No. 4011, Feb. 8, 1980, p. 143.

in the Hellenic pantheon, Dionysus came to be considered one of the most important dieties of Olympus. This was because he gradually became the focus for mystic ideas which made him one of the few immortals who might be approached for hope and consolation. An illegitimate son of Zeus, Dionysus suffered many vicissitudes as a child owing to Hera's jealousy, but eventually he took the place that was rightly his on Olympus. Grown to manhood Dionysus discovered the vine and ivy plant whose perennial hardiness was taken as a symbol for continuity of life. Like the vine, ivy can produce a certain state of euphoria if chewed, so Dionysus became the god of intoxicating plants, the god who loved joy and merry tumult. He would go surrounded by his thiasos (procession of persons dancing and singing in honor of a god); in this instance, a procession of satyrs and maenads who would dance to the sound of the flute and the tambourine. Inspired by the thiasos, in the course of certain festivals, women succumbed to enthusiasm and ran through the forests in wild, bloody delirium (cf. Euripides' *Bacchae*).

Sixth and fifth century vases often bear paintings representing the thiasos. One notes that in the midst of these wild processions. Dionysus is shown standing calm and majestic, wearing a long and richly embroidered robe, his face framed by a majestic beard. In the fifth century he became a god of the dead, whose survival he ensured, perhaps because he was already the diety of plants whose existence shows such tenacity. About the same time a more romantic depiction became popular and he was shown as a beautiful, naked young man with long ringlets falling to his shoulders, bearing away Ariadne. But this image was considered as a symbolic representation of the god leading a mortal soul to immortality.

The religious policy pursued by the tyrants in the sixth century strongly forwarded the cult of Dionysus, "the god of the peasants, the looser of care and grief, the great transformer."[8] When the state took control, the disorderly

[8]Albin Lesky, *A History of Greek Literature*, (New York: Thomas Y. Crowell, 1966), p. 227.

rites were soon limited. The most important festival at
Athens was the Greater or City Dionysia, held in the month
of Elaphebelion (March/April). In this connection Dionysus was called Eleuthereus, since the festival had been
brought from the village Eleutherae. At the same time a
temple was built for Dionysus on the southern slope of the
Acropolis. The festival started with a procession on the
road to Eleutherae and then back to the temple, from which
the statue of the god was taken to the theater by the *ephebes*.
During this procession the dithyramb, the song sung in
service of Dionysus, was performed by choirs which
included satyrs. It was from this dithyramb that tragedy
and comedy developed.

Introduction of Dialogue

This development came about through the gradual
introduction of dialogue into the choral odes of the original
ritual. First, songs attached to hero-cults were introduced.
In this way the myth, after its epic and choral-lyric phase,
entered on its tragic phase in which poets made it the
vehicle of ethical and religious problems. Thus, "in the
course of its development the choral ode came to include
themes presupposing more and more knowledge on the part
of the audience. It was an obvious step to prepare the
hearers for what was coming by means of a prologue.
Similarly a sequence of choral odes dealing with the various
phases of a mythical narrative could be made possible by the
simple device of bringing on a speaker between two odes.
The next step was to have the narrator and the chorus-
leader speaking to each other."[9]

The institution of competitions of tragedies at the Great
or City Dionysia, the principal festival in honor of the god
Dionysus, began to be held at Athens in 534 B.C. It became
the custom to illustrate three successive episodes from the
same legend. Each of these episodes constituted a tragedy
and together they made up a linked trilogy. Then came a

[9]*Ibid.*, p. 228.

fourth play which was especially related to the Dionysus legend, as the chorus was formed by satyrs, the companions of Dionysus. This play became the satyric drama and so the drama cycle because a tetralogy, but this was not preserved for long. Aeschylus added a second actor (*deuteroagonistes*) and Sophocles a third (*tritoagonistes*); Greek drama rarely used more than three actors. In the course of time Greek tragedies began to follow a more or less standard pattern, consisting of: prologue, complication, recognition scene, and denouement. In 486 B.C. comedies began to appear in the program of the Great Dionysia.

The Great Dionysia developed into one of the great cultural phenomena of human history, involving as it did practically the entire population in one way or another and the staging of a dozen or more original dramas within a few days. H. D. F. Kitto has written that "Athens from (say) 480 to 380 was clearly the most civilized society that has yet existed."[10]

Tragedy and Comedy

Both tragedy and comedy arose from the cult of Dionysus, therefore from essentially the same kind of death and resurrection ritual. Tragedy emphasizes conflict and death, comedy resurrection and marriage. They can deal with the same situations, but from different perspectives and with different emphases. Dealing with man as a social being, the dramatist is aware that he is in the presence of a contradiction—a rational-animal; that behind the social being lurks an animal being. Comedy celebrates the latter. Tragedy depicts the duality as a fatal contradiction in the nature of things, while comedy depicts it as one more instance of the incongruous reality that every man must live with as best he can. Wherever there is contradiction, the comical is present (S. Kierkegaard). The tragic is a suffering contradiction, the comic a painless contradiction. Comedy

[10]*The Greeks*, (New York: Penguin Books, 1957), p. 96.

is painless because it shows a way out while tragedy does not. Comedy has a U-shaped plot, with the action sinking into deep and often potentially tragic complications, and then suddenly turning upward into a happy ending.

In the minds of some, tragedy revolves around the concepts of the so-called "tragic flaw" and character development, but these do not seem to have been important elements in classical Greek tragedy.

In comedy the protagonist is often an *eiron* (ironical man) who feigns stupidity and makes himself out to be less than he is. But in the end his humility proves to be wisdom. Contrasted with him is the *alazon* or imposter—a boastful, foolish, pretender. Often the reader (hearer) is admitted to the real world from the beginning, is given knowledge hidden from the characters in the story. The story operates on two levels, and this sets up ironic, incongruous situations. Things are often not what they seem, and characters make ridiculously false judgments.

CHAPTER 3
DRAMA AND
BIBLICAL WRITINGS

THE TWO BOOKS OF THE BIBLE that have been most consistently brought into conjunction with Greek drama are Job and Mark. In Job the reader is informed at the outset regarding the circumstances of Job's trials, knowledge that is withheld from his "friends," so that they are soon cutting ridiculous figures, and eventually Job is justified and restored. In the first verse of his gospel Mark informs his readers as to who Jesus is, knowledge that is withheld from the disciples, so that their conduct is characterized by non-understanding and failure throughout the gospel, but Jesus rises from the grave and reestablishes contact with those same disciples.

Theodore of Mopsuestia gave it as his opinion that Job was a deliberate imitation of Greek tragedy. In the sixteenth century Theodore Beza began a course of lectures on Job in Geneva by dividing the book into acts and scenes, and in the eighteenth century Bishop Lowth, whose theory of Hebrew poetry was to prove so influential, tells us that virtually all scholars regarded Job as a drama and discussed it as they would a Greek tragedy. The voice out of the whirlwind in Job has the same effect as the *deus ex machina* used in classical Greek drama. This theatrical device will also figure in our discussion of the ending of Mark's gospel.

Almost Universal Diffusion

Whether the author of Mark lived in Galilee or Southern Syria (a common and growing opinion) or in Rome (a much older tradition) there is a good reason to believe that he would have been acquainted with Greek drama; to such an extent had Greek culture penetrated to all parts of the Mediterranean world, both east and west. Tragedy was born and flourished in Athens, but it rapidly spread throughout the entire Hellenistic world. By virtue of its early association with the worship of Dionysus, drama became a regular feature of religious festivals wherever they were held in the Greek-speaking world. By the time of Alexander the Great drama was co-extensive with the Bacchic worship; it had penetrated into every region of the world in which the Greek language was spoken. When tragedy became disassociated from its religious roots, it acquired a quasi-universal popularity spreading from France and Italy in the west to Syria and Phoenicia in the east. An enormous number of Greek theaters was erected in a continuous series from Sicily to Phoenicia. Guilds of actors were organized in France, Italy, Sicily, Cyprus, Lydia, Galatia, Ptolemais (Acco) in Palestine.

Greek tragedy implanted itself so firmly in Italy that it survived there long after it became extinct almost everywhere else. It also gave birth to Latin drama, which in turn made a decisive impact upon the theater of Europe and England up to modern times. When the Romans conquered southern Italy (early third century B.C.) they encountered highly cultured Greek cities, and the presence of a substantial Greek population in Rome later facilitated the adoption of tragic drama as an essential part of the cultural life of the city. Mention is made of contests in Greek tragedy as late as the second century A.D., and during the fifth century in Constantinople.

In Rome most of the representations took place on occasions of official festivities and attendance was open to the general public. Nothing would have prevented a man like Mark from being present at such performances. "The enduring success of Greek tragedy in the Roman world, including the city of Rome, was such that a person sufficiently conversant with cultural endeavors to undertake a project like writing the Gospel of Mark would have had at least a general acquaintance with it, such as was accessible to the common man, especially if he was literate in Greek—as Mark was."[1]

Significant developments also took place in Greek tragedy's immediate progeny, the Latin drama. Departing from mythological themes, Latin dramatists also wrote historical plays based on contemporary events. Demand for tragic performances in the first century of our era propelled gifted actors to fame and wealth. In the reign of Augustus, the rage for tragedy had developed almost into a mania, and some dramas had been written by the emperor himself. Particularly significant was the prevalence during Mark's time of a kind of tragedy specifically written not for stage presentation, but simply for reading—the literary or closet drama.

An Enduring Aesthetic Form

In summary it can be said then that "in Mark's time, tragedies in the classical style were still being written in both Greek and Latin, in the city of Rome as well as in other parts of the Graeco-Roman world. Likewise, tragedies—old and new, Greek and Latin—were performed on the stage of Rome and elsewhere. Moreover, a long-standing tradition was revived in Mark's day of tragedies composed in the classical form, but for reading rather than staging. Of such narrative-tragedies, ten that were probably written during the same decade as Mark's Gospel have been

[1]Gilbert G. Bilezikian, *The Liberated Gospel*, A Comparison of the Gospel of Mark and Greek Tragedy, (Grand Rapids: Baker Book House, 1977), p. 38.

preserved, one of which is a historical drama recounting events that had taken place during the author's lifetime."[2]

Actual attendance would not be required if this were precluded by Mark's Jewish background. Sufficient knowedge of the classics was available in common report. It is no more necessary to suppose that the author of Mark actually attended Greek plays than to believe that Paul's references to the theater, the gymnasium, and the stadium, imply that he was in frequent attendance. The writer of Mark had an acquaintance with the Greek drama such as was the common possession of anyone who was intelligently responsive to the values of Hellenistic civilization. The probability of Mark being familiar with tragedy, the dominant literary form of the culture in whose language he composed his own work, cannot be lightly dismissed.

Working with the gospel traditions that had come down to him, Mark shaped them according to a compatible model available in Greek tragedy, "the most influential and enduring aesthetic form designed by men to portray the great dilemmas of existence, and the torments brought upon mortals by their mysterious passions."[3]

Pattern of Tragedy

The action in tragedy follows a general pattern. First, a potentially tragic situation is sketched and the significance of the hero is suggested. A series of events follows which precipitates a climax in the action, usually a recognition scene. The true nature or identity of the hero is dimly perceived in the play, although it has been clearly manifested to the spectator-reader. Subsequently the forces threatening the hero redouble their efforts to bring disaster. But while the situation changes for the worse, the determination of the hero remains unshaken. Finally comes the resolution of the action when the forces set against the hero seem to crush him.

[2]*Ibid.*, p. 48.
[3]*Ibid.*, p. 34.

Mark quite clearly divides into two parts at 8:27-30, Peter's confession of Jesus' messiahship at Caesarea Philippi. The gospel differs before and after that point in a number of easily observable respects. The first half is taken up largely with Jesus' miracles; these attract followers to him but also stir up bitter opposition; Jesus' adversaries are usually referred to as Pharisees. In the second half, Jesus' teaching predominates, and the key element in that teaching is that it is necessary for Jesus to suffer and die; Jesus' adversaries during this phase are designated as "the chief priests and the elders and the scribes"; Jesus is progressively deserted by his followers so that in the end he is in a state of almost total abandonment.

But can the story of Jesus, which ends with a resurrection, be cast in the form of a tragedy? Contrariwise, can the story of Jesus, with its exalted seriousness, be cast in the form of a comedy? Here it may help to recall how tragedy and comedy originated.

Tragedy is Basic

The competition in tragedies had been going at Athens for fifty years before comedy was admitted. Tragedy was realized with some fullness before there was time for comedy. And comedy was secondary and derivative in another sense. Tragedies were presented as trilogies, three related plays, to which comedy (a satire play) was added as a fourth. The comedy used the same material which had just been treated tragically but turned it upside down in the form of a parody. The comic began as a burlesque of the solemn and sacred. Comedy repairs an omission, provides a correction. After three periods of reverent seriousness, the animal man demands some diversion. He invites comedy to make a joke of the tragic experience he has just had. Since comedy grew out of tragedy there is something in it that is not funny, and, in fact, comic, "happy" endings usually contain some contretemps.

Christopher Fry, the contemporary dramatist, tells us

that when he sets out to write a comedy the idea first presents itself to him as tragedy;[4] Walter Kerr, the drama critic, decided to write a book on comedy, to which he is passionately devoted, only to find that "tragedy—most stubbornly—persisted in getting in the way."[5] These experiences indicate that tragedy is basic and comedy an afterthought, a completion.

While comedy is sorry for man, tragedy sings his praises. There is never anything mean, undignified, or undesirable in the goal of a tragic action; there is a bias toward good in the turn of the tragic wheel.

And it is simply not true that tragedy must have an unhappy ending. If we can judge by the one complete trilogy we have (Aeschylus' *Oresteia*) the trilogy as a whole does not end in unrelieved disaster. A first agony gives birth to a second and a second to a third, but this third play acts as an ultimate discharge of pain and responsibility, ending in reconciliation. Even in single plays we find hints of justice done and reconciliation achieved.

If tragedy can be reduced to a number of elements, the last would have to be an affirmation. Some think that these elements are four: an act of shame or horror, suffering, knowledge, and affirmation or reaffirmation. The basic pattern of tragedy may be schematized as "the act of shame which precipitates the suffering which generates the knowledge which issues in the affirmation."[6]

The next to the last of these elements is also important for our purposes. This knowledge which springs from suffering must be a knowledge that has the property of illuminating some fundamental aspect of man's nature or the human condition. It may, but need not, take the form of self-knowledge. What matters in tragedy is not that the

[4]*Comedy*, in Robert W. Corrigan and James L. Losenberg, *The Art of the Theatre,* a Critical Anthology of Drama, (San Francisco: Chandler, 1964), p. 380.

[5]*Tragedy and Comedy*, (New York: Simon and Schuster, 1967), p. 13.

[6]Dorothea Krook, *The Elements of Tragedy*, (New Haven/London: Yale University Press, 1969), p. 9.

tragic hero should receive the knowledge issuing from the suffering, but that we, the readers or audience, should receive it.

This situation fits Mark's purposes perfectly. He has a vision of Christianity and he wants to impart this "knowledge" to his readers. He does this by the way he structures his narrative of Jesus' ministry.

CHAPTER 4
SOME LITERARY THEORY AND A
FIRST RAPID SURVEY

THE AIM OF BIBLICAL LITERARY CRITICISM is to analyze biblical writings using language and procedures that literary critics can understand. Not that there is one uniform terminology in literary criticism, but a foundation is provided by the writings of Plato and Aristotle. Thus, at one point in his *Poetics* Aristotle says: I now want to treat of narrative (*diegesis*) which is in meter (what we would call "epic"). Then he goes on to say that the *story* (*mythos*) should be construed "round a single piece of action, whole and complete in itself, with a beginning (*arche*), middle (*mesa*), and end (*telos*)." XXII:23. Here Aristotle is treating of *narrative*, the concept in terms of which basically we shall analyze Mark's gospel in this work.

All literature focuses on storytelling or narrative; the urge to "tell a story" is the paradigmatic urge which results in getting literary creation onto paper. A child's earliest experience of protracted verbal art forms is normally experience of stories. Literature can be focused on narrative because narrative enjoys a kind of primacy among literary forms, and indeed among the oral forms which preceded literature and out of which literature grew. Narrative is the primal way in which the human lifeworld is organized verbally and intellectually. As Walter Ong, S.J., has written: "All knowledge is grounded in experience; experience is strung out in time; time sequence calls for narrative."[1]

In his *Poetics* Aristotle says that he will treat of *narrative* (*diegesis*) and then tells us what *story* (*mythos*) should be. This intimate connection between narrative and story is still found in literary theory today. Narrative is embodied in *story* and *discourse*. Story is the *what* of narrative and discourse is the *way* or *how*; story is the *content*, discourse the *expression* of narrative. Story is the continuum of events presupposing the total set of all conceivable details, and in their "proper" order (logical or chronological). Discourse chooses which events and objects to actually state and which to imply, and determines in what order they shall be related.

Story and Discourse

The story line is longer than the discourse line; and people on the story line know more than people on the discourse line (the reader knows more than the characters involved in the action). Narrative may appear in a variety of materializing media: verbal (including drama, tragedy or comedy), cinematic, balletic, musical, pantomimic, or whatever. Aristotle said that a story should have a beginning, a middle, and an end. When the story is presented as a drama the terms *complication, recognition,* and *denouement* come into use.

Mark divides into two parts at 8:27-30, Peter's confession of Jesus' messiahship at Caesarea Philippi, which can rightly be called a recognition. Combining the elements encountered to this point, Mark's narrative looks like this:

[1]*Interfaces of the Word*, (Ithaca: Cornell University Press, 1977), 244-45.

Isa.

40:3   RECOGNITION

STORY   Complication   Denouement   Parousia

MIDPOINT

8:27

DISCOURSE   John   Jesus   Empty Tomb

An important characteristic of narrative is that story and discourse represent two levels of information. The story level is comprised of all events described or referred to in the narrative, but in their casual and logical sequence, whereas the plotting of this world (discourse level) is to be seen in the ways its components have been selected and arranged in a sequence of narrated incidents.

Mark's Narrative

The reader knows more than the characters in the plotted narrative. In the title, 1:1, the narrator tells the narratee who Jesus is. When the discourse gets under way it becomes evident that the characters in the story do not share this knowledge. Two time frames are superimposed in the narrative: that of the reader and that of the characters in the plotted narrative.

The title is followed by a Scripture quotation. Mark writes: "As it is written in Isaiah the prophet," but then proceeds to quote Malachi 3:1 ("Behold, I send my messenger before thy face, who shall prepare thy way") and then gives the quote from Isaiah, "The voice of one crying in the wilderness." Thus Mark gets a bracket (one of his favorite literary devices) into the first verse of his work. Both quotes refer to John the Baptist but John and Jesus are closely associated. The Malachi quote is also a *foreshadowing*, another much used Markan device. When Jesus cleanses the temple the reader will recall that Malachi also speaks of the "messenger" coming suddenly to his temple (3:1), and at the end of the gospel the women are to remind the disciples that Jesus is "going before them" to Galilee. Thus the beginning and the end of the gospel are linked up.

In the opening verses of the gospel we also see a series of predictions, not all of which are fulfilled in the plotted narrative. Isaiah makes a prediction that is fulfilled in John the Baptist. John predicts that a Mightier One would come, and this is fulfilled in the appearance of Jesus. John also predicts that Jesus would baptize with the Spirit, but this is nowhere fulfilled in the plotted narrative. This is one of the events spoken of in the plotted narrative which takes place after the end of the plotted narrative.

Just when the public ministry is set to get underway the narrative makes a reference to John's fate: he is Jesus' precursor in the manner of his death also; another foreshadowing. Jesus announces that the Kingdom of God *eggiken*; it is both a present and a future reality. Jesus' calling of the first disciples already indicates what discipleship should be like. This is an anticipation of the explicit teaching on discipleship which characterizes the second half of the gospel.

Jesus' preaching and miracles win him followers but very quickly their lack of understanding appears. When Jesus goes off to the "lonely place" to pray, Peter goes to call him back. In the light of how things developed later, one senses that Peter was thinking that Jesus could be using his time more profitably, performing other and perhaps more striking messianic signs. If this was the case, this would be the first instance of the disciples' failure to understand what kind of messiah Jesus was. By 2:16 the scribes of the Pharisees are questioning his practices and by 3:6 Jesus' opponents are planning "how to destroy him."

Insiders/Outsiders

Next, even Jesus' followers are divided into insiders and outsiders, a line of division that runs through family (see Chapter 12). The division between insider/outsider appears at the end of Chapter 3 to be taken up again in the Purpose of the Parables passage. This in turn is followed by another reference to the disciples' incomprehension; indeed, more than a reference, an exclamation of surprise: "Do you not understand this parable? How then will you understand all the parables?" (4:13). The insiders are given the Mystery of the Kingdom and additional private instruction. Nonetheless, the reader is warned that even those who have been called can be susceptible to spiritual myopia.

As they stand in the present text the three main parables of Mark 4 (Sower, Seed Growing Secretly, Mustard Seed) give what J. Jeremias calls the Great Assurance. Doubts have been rising in the minds of the disciples. Can this Jesus really be the Messiah? In many ways his message and ministry were not what had been expected, and there was the bitter opposition he was stirring up. The parables say: despite all appearances to the contrary (and there are many), the Kingdom of God is at hand and will achieve its effect. When seed is sown, much is lost, but a crop is produced; even when men observe nothing and are doing nothing, the seed is growing; from a tiny seed a great plant appears.

The non-understanding of the disciples is the theme which ties together the material between Chapter 4 and the middle of the gospel. Complaints about incomprehension steadily increase and peak at 6:52: "They did not understand about the loaves, but their hearts were hardened." Non-understanding is found in four passages, and clustered around these references are three other significant elements: a bread or feeding miracle, a miracle on the sea (calming the storm), and withdrawal into Gentile territory.

In Mark a plotted incident may have a backward or forward reference. We find references to events that occur before or after the incident (unit) in which the reference occurs. After Jesus had expelled several demons, he is accused of doing this by a demonic power. Jesus repudiates the idea and goes on to say that demons can be driven out only after Satan has been bound. Now Jesus has been driving demons out since shortly after the temptation; therefore, within Mark's narrative world, Jesus' temptation (1:13) would seem to be the occasion on which Satan was bound.

From 4:10-12 on, the suspense about the Kingdom is suspense about the disciples' privileged knowledge of it, but also about their ignorance of Jesus' identity. The non-understanding passages are explicit backward references. The reader is required to reflect back to previously plotted incidents, both to understand those incidents, and what has transpired between them and the incidents in which the backward reference occurs. The failure of the disciples to understand something in one incident is treated as the result of their failure to understand something in earlier incidents.

In the Purpose of the Parables passage (4:10-12) the disciples are given the "secret of the Kingdom of God." The non-understanding passages emphasize the disciples' failure to understand the secret they have received—whatever that secret may be. Despite their privileged information they understand no more than others (cf. 4:10-13, 7:18). The poetic combination of the forward movement of episodes with the backward references of some of them serves to involve the reader in a developing plot.

Literary Dynamics

In 1979 Menakhen Perry, an Israeli critic, labeled this back and forth movement of a narrative "Literary Dynamics." In an article entitled "Literary Dynamics, How the Order of a Text Creates its Meanings," Perry shows that the meaning of a narrative is not exhausted by the *static* sum total of its elements. "The effects of the entire reading process all contribute to the meaning of the work: its surprises; the changes along the way; the process of a gradual, zig-zag-like build-up of meanings, their reinforcement, development, revision and replacement; the relations between expectations aroused at one stage of the text and discoveries actually made in subsequent stages; the process of retrospective re-patterning and even the peculiar survival of meanings which were first constructed and then rejected."[2] One sometimes suspects that Mark was ordering his material according to some of these principles. Of necessity, narrative is linear, strung out. Its verbal elements appear one after another, and its complexes, so-called semantic complexes (scenes, ideas, characters, plot, value-judgments), build up cumulatively, through adjustments and readjustments. A literary text does not yield its information all at once but successively. And this is not just an unfortunate consequence of the linear character of language. Authors can effectively utilize the fact that their material is grasped successively and the ordering and distribution of the elements in a text can suggest the meaning or even alternate meanings. Mark exemplifies this in the form of brackets, foreshadowings, repetitions, and backward references.

Recognition

After the second feeding miracle Jesus again passes into Gentile territory and heals a blind man at Bethsaida, Peter's home town (a second healing of a blind man comes at the end of the journey to Jerusalem). At Caesaria Philippi Peter recognizes Jesus as Messiah. Jesus immediately brings the concept of Son of Man into conjunction with messiahship. On the journey to Jerusalem which follows, three times Jesus predicts his passion, but Peter and the other disciples are unable to take in what he is saying. Jesus' entry into Jerusalem is greeted by uncertain acclamations (some hail him as Messiah, others as eschatological prophet). The cleansing of the temple (bracketed by the cursing of the fig tree) portends the coming destruction of the temple and this is underlined by the parable of the Vineyard.

In his Farewell Address Jesus sets forth what life will

[2] *Poetics Today*, 1(1979), 41.

be like between the Resurrection and the Parousia. It will be a time when he will be absent, when the disciples will have to undergo great trial and persecution. But it is also a time when the disciples will give up their former error and incomprehension and they will become heralds of the Kingdom.

Jesus' Farewell Address ends with a ringing exhortation to vigilance: "Take heed, watch; for you do not know when the time will come," (vs. 33); "And what I say to you I say to all: Watch," (vs. 37). Yet after the Last Supper in the garden of Gethsemane, after renewed admonitions to vigilance, Jesus comes to the disciples three times and finds them asleep every time. When Jesus is arrested all the disciples flee, one even without his clothes, the very embodiment of fleeing disciples.

Peter tags along on the edge of the crowd into the court-yard of the high priest. While Jesus' trial is taking place in the courtroom at the hands of the highest authorities of the land, Peter's trial is taking place in the courtyard at the hands of one of the maids of the high priest. When Jesus dies, the curtain of the temple is torn in two from top to bottom, a portent of the coming destruction, which Jesus had foretold.

At the conclusion of Mark's discourse the women go to the tomb and find it empty. The young man instructs them to go and tell the disciples that Jesus is going before them and that they will see him there, as he has told them. The women flee from the tomb trembling with astonishment. And they say nothing to anyone, for they are afraid.

Narrative as Discourse

Such then is Mark's narrative in discourse. By his title "The beginning of the gospel of Jesus Christ, the Son of God," (1:1) he accomplishes two important things: he indicates his audience (the addressee), and he establishes two levels of comprehension (what the reader knows and what the characters in the story know). Prefixing no infancy narrative, he breaks into the middle of things. This means that he presupposes a great deal. He presupposes that his readers understand what he means by Christ (Messiah) and Son of God. It follows that Mark is writing for a Christian audience, an already believing audience. Since the narrative is *about* the disciples, they are not the addressees, leaving only the Christians as possible candidates for this role. The reader knows who Jesus is; vs. 1 tells him that. The disciples do not have that information when they are first called nor is their non-understanding completely dispelled at any point in plotted time. This difference of knowledge, a characteristic device of Greek drama, sets up many incongruous, ironic situations.

As a culmination of a "good news of salvation" the ending of Mark's gospel is as paradoxical as anyone could wish, ending as it does on a note of trembling and astonishment, a disregarded command, and fear. Mark's unusual ending is a device to transfer the mystery and ambiguity which is a pronounced element on the level of plotted time (time of the characters in the narrative) to the level of the reader, who may have felt superior to the doubting disciples all the way through the gospel. But now he is surrounded by the same ambiguity and mystery; will his response be any better?

CHAPTER 5

MARKAN STYLE

SINCE 1850 MARK'S GOSPEL has attracted a great deal of attention, at first because of the discussion about its possible priority, but before that it was largely the neglected gospel. The first commentary comes from the fifth century, followed by others in the eighth and twelfth. This neglect was due perhaps more than anything else to the idea that Mark was just an abbreviation of Matthew; then Matthew was an apostle, while Mark was not. But there are also signs that readers have always found Mark puzzling; they have never known what to make of him. At one time or another every one of the four evangelical symbols was assigned to Mark, which betrays uncertainty about its meaning.

Mark is characterized by indirect communication; not much of the teaching is communicated directly. Then Mark is a close-knit whole; you have to see the whole to see any part of it. Even if Matthew's gospel was not written first, it is not at all surprising that it ended up in first place in the New Testament canon. For the purpose of practical use Matthew proved far superior to Mark. The arrangement of the material in the interests of oral teaching and easy retention in the memory which reaches its fullest development in Matthew, is much less obvious in Mark. "The

Person and portrait of the Lord," R. H. Lightfoot has written, "as offered for our reverent contemplation and worship in Matthew, is likely to be more intelligible and attractive to catholic churchmen, when we recall their devotion to law and order and precise definition, than the Person and the portrait, deeply human it is true, but also profoundly mysterious and baffling, in the pages of Mark."[1]

The qualities which Mark's narrative possesses are due in part at least to the fact that he was following a dramatic pattern. As we have seen already, a playwright who turns to the novel is at an advantage because he has learned to be brief, has learned not to linger on the way, but to stick to his point and get on with his story.

Auerbach's Mimesis

These qualities bring Mark to mind. And Mark could all the more easily use them because they are characteristic of much biblical writing. In his *Mimesis*, Eric Auerbach draws our attention to what a strong parallel there is between Mark and a very typical example of Old Testament narrative, the Binding of Isaac, Genesis 22. "After these things God tested Abraham, and said to him, 'Abraham!' And he said, 'Here am I.'" The lack of descriptive detail is particularly striking. We are not told where we are, whence or how Yahweh has made himself manifest, or why he is tempting Abraham. Abraham answers: "Hinne-ni, Behold me!" not an indication of actual place but of moral position in respect to God. "Here I am awaiting your command." The two speakers are not on the same level: Abraham's words and gestures are directed toward the depths of the picture and upward.

In the rest of the story, nothing involved is described. They are serving-man, ass, wood, and knife, and nothing else, without an epithet. We are told nothing about the

---

[1] *The Gospel Message of St. Mark*, (London: Oxford University Press, 1950), pp. 2-3.

journey except that it took three days, and even that in a mysterious way. Abraham rose "early in the morning" (vs. 3) which bespeaks resolution, promptness, punctual obedience and "on the third day he lifted up his eyes and saw the place afar off," (vs. 4) with still plenty of time to climb the mountain. Isaac is the only element that receives an appositive: "Take your son, your only son Isaac whom you love," (vs. 2). Isaac "may be handsome or ugly, intelligent or stupid, tall or short, pleasant or unpleasant—we are not told. Only what we need to know about him as a personage in the action, here and now, is illuminated, so that it may become apparent how terrible Abraham's temptation is, and that God is fully aware of it."[2]

Arresting starkness of foreground, an enormous height of background, are beautifully illustrated by the Binding of Isaac passage, characterized as it is by a high degree of internalization, timelessness, colorless backdrop, suppression of feeling in a speechless drama. There are other types of narrative in the Bible, to be sure, but the Binding of Isaac is of a type that is characteristic and it may well remind one of Mark's portrait of Jesus. Mark illuminates only what we need to know about Jesus in the action of a particular incident.

Mark presupposes that the reader knows the main outline of Jesus' life. "We learn nothing, except incidentally, of his home, upbringing, or appearance; we are not told his age, when he began to teach; we hardly ever see him, except as a teacher or mighty worker or engaged in controversy; above all, we are not admitted to a knowledge of his inner life."[3] Mark is not interested in giving us a complete version of Jesus' teaching. We sense that he could if he wanted to but that this was not his object.

In Mark the visual and the sensory is rarely completely realized; it appears because it is attached to the events

[2]Erich Auerbach, *Mimesis. The Representation of Reality in Western Literature*, (Princeton: Princeton University Press, 1953), pp. 10-11.

[3]R. H. Lightfoot, *History and Interpretation of the Gospels,* (New York: Harper and Bros.), p. 66.

which are to be related. So much remains unexpressed, unexplained. There is so much that Mark does not tell us, so much that the modern reader would like to know. The scene depicting Peter's denial ends abruptly with no indication of what happened to this Peter who, as Mark's readers would have been expected to know, became one of the giants in the Christian movement. How was he accepted back into the ranks of the disciples? Mark reports only that statement made by the "young man" at the tomb that the women are to tell "the disciples and Peter" that Jesus is going before them to Galilee (16:7). But the women disobey the command, and the reader never learns whether the disciples ever went to Galilee. To those who view Mark as a piece of historical writing in which the intent is to describe events accurately and fully, it obviously must appear deficient.

The Double Trial

The story of Peter's denial (14:66-72) illustrates two characteristics of Mark's gospel: two levels of meaning, and irony. Jesus' trial before the Sanhedrin is bracketed or framed by the account of Peter's denial. In 14:54 it is reported that "Peter had followed Jesus at a distance, right into the courtyard of the high priest." Once it is established that Peter is below in the courtyard the narrative returns to the scene where Jesus is being interrogated by the high priest (14:55). Following the interrogation and the rendering of the verdict against Jesus, "some began to spit on him, saying to him, 'Prophesy!'." Immediately, the narrative once again switches to Peter in the courtyard below. There Peter is questioned by the maid of the high priest. Richly ironic relationships are thereby established and the difference between what the reader knows and what the characters in the narrative know comes across strongly.

In Greek drama the *eiron* is the man who depreciates himself, who is more than he seems, while the *alazon* is the boaster. According to Northrop Frye irony "indicates a technique of appearing to be less than one is, which in literature becomes most commonly a technique of saying as little and meaning as much as possible, or, in a more general way, a pattern of words that turn away from direct statement, or its own obvious meaning."[4]

Neither Peter nor any of the other characters are aware of the "real" meaning of the events in which they are involved. But the reader can glimpse that real meaning if he is attentive, and if he does he cannot miss the irony of the situation. While Jesus is mocked as a false prophet one of his prophecies is being fulfilled in the courtyard. While Jesus openly acknowledges the truth about himself even though it means death, Peter, to escape death, denies that he knows Jesus—even invoking a curse upon himself.

The story of Peter's denial operates on two levels. There is the level of the bare sensory perception of the events that take place, the level to which both reader and characters, alike, have access. There is also the level of the deeper meaning of the events to which only the reader has access. And for Mark it is the meaning at this level that moves him to tell the story. At the deeper level of the story the reader sees that quite often things are not what they seem.

Two Time Frames

The two levels of meaning arise from the superimposition of two time frames: that of Jesus and his contemporaries and that of Mark and his Christian readers. These latter know who Jesus is from the first verse of the gospel. Throughout the gospel they observe Jesus' disciples struggling to recognize Jesus as the Messiah in the unlikely events of his life which hide his identity, an ambiguity which can be overcome only by faith. By the same token there are two levels of meaning: what is accessible to the Christian reader and what is accessible to the characters

---

[4]*Anatomy of Criticism*, (Princeton: Princeton University Press), p. 40.

involved in the story.

By the time the Christian reader comes to the end of the gospel he is made to realize that he too is confronted by a challenge to faith. Mark accomplishes this by his unusual ending: the women fled from the tomb, "for they were afraid," (16:8). The superimposition of the two time frames is so handled that the reader is confronted by the same challenge to faith as were Jesus' contemporaries.

Mark's message is primarily for his Christian readers. Will they do any better than the disciples? These Christians are facing their own trials, and they cannot see God's hand in what is happening to them any more than the disciples could. But things are still not as they seem. Despite all contrary appearances, God's Kingdom is moving towards its consummation, and in God's time all will see the Son of Man exalted. It is possible Mark's Christian readers too can be caught up in decisive, history transforming events and be as blind to the situation as the characters in Mark's gospel.

The Literary Perspective

The message of Mark's gospel comes across most clearly from a literary perspective. When we do this we work with literary phenomena for which a literary explanation must be given in any case. Such a study is necessary and valid however one views pre-Markan tradition and its use; it is valid even if the gospel has undergone successive stages of redaction. In this way a number of problems in the narrative may be solved already on the literary level, without recourse to hypothetical source reconstruction or psychological analysis of the characters in the story, reconstructions that not many people can or care to follow. This approach takes seriously the possibility that Mark, the final redactor of the story, can at least be credited with the ability to tell a coherent story.

At many points it becomes evident that Mark is working with traditions which have reached him in the form of complexes. Still there is enough continuity in style and theme to indicate the presence of structure and cohesiveness. Mark has real impact on the traditions he uses. He makes selections of what should be included from tradition, he edits the traditions in a particular fashion, he adds narrative framework and interpretative comments. All this would seem to indicate that before one can inquire into the question of the history of traditions and sources one must first inquire of the material at the level of its present literary form. This sort of interest is further encouraged when we find that Mark's gospel as a whole is characterized by literary cohesiveness.

A methodological approach, then, that makes every effort to determine the place of a particular text within the whole of the gospel is a sound one. Only when we have failed to account for the presence of a text or to provide a reasonable account of its function within the story are we justified in seeking explanations for the text based on Mark's unthinking use of prior tradition. The case is that we do in fact find cohesiveness and structure in Mark's gospel. Therefore it is both appropriate and necessary to begin the study of Mark at a literary level, inquiring about the function of each part in the whole of Mark's gospel and noting Markan themes and style.

CHAPTER 6

CONCENTRIC DEVELOPMENT

AGAINST THE BACKGROUND of what has been said about the history of drama and about literary theory, we may now approach the most thoroughgoing study of Mark's literary background. This is the work of a Belgian Benedictine, Benoit Standaert, presented as a thesis at the Catholic University of Nijmegen in 1978, entitled *L'Evangile selon Marc: Composition et Genre Litteraire*.[1]

Over a period of 100 years (1875-1975) at least eight critics have sought in ancient dramatic art the model explaining the literary character of Mark. Striking is the fact that most often these writers undertook their inquiries independently of one another. All had some knowledge of ancient classical literature.

Central to Standaert's work are a few ideas which he uses very effectively. By Mark's time the dramatic, rhetorical, and historical genres were well-blended. Orators and historians were striving to be dramatic, and dramatists were using rhetorical devices and incorporating contemporary events into their plays.[2] This blending of genres produced the *concentric development*. A literary work should

[1](Brugge: Sint-Andreisabdij, 1978).

[2]Cf., R. Scholes and R. Kellogg, *The Nature of Narrative*, (New York: Oxford University Press, 1966), pp. 61-62.

begin and end in the same way, with similar material (and so should smaller passages within the work), with the most important material in the middle. Typically, such a unit will being and end with narrative material between which discourse material will be framed. Furthermore, passages should not be simply juxtaposed, strung together, without connecting links. From the rhetoricians dramatists borrow the principle that passages should be "mixed and tied together by their ends" (Lucian); each part should be prepared for by "seeds of proof sown" in the preceding part (Quintilian). One thinks, of course, of Mark's use of the frame or bracket, and the way, for example, that he prepares for Chapter 4 by references to parables and a division between insiders and outsiders at the end of Chapter 3.

In his *Poetics* Aristotle lays it down that a narrative should be constructed "round a single piece of action, whole and complete in itself, with a beginning (*arche*), middle (*mesa*), and end (*telos*)," XXII:23. If we add a *prologue* and an *epilogue*, this fairly well covers what has ever been said about the essential parts of narrative. There have been changes of terminology as this basic distinction was applied to different kinds of narrative but the essentials remain the same. Terminologies were elaborated for drama (tragedy and comedy), oratory (rhetoric, discourse) and history. But by Mark's time these disciplines had become well mixed.

We have already seen the terms *complication, recognition,* and *denouement* applied to Mark. The recognition was Peter's confession at Caesarea Philippi. Looked at from the perspective of concentric development, the recognition proves to be part of a longer central unit, and the most important, as is usual with the central unit. Standaert follows the terminology of Quintilian, a highly successful teacher of rhetoric in Rome for twenty years after A.D. 68. The three main parts of a literary development are called *narration, argumentation,* and *denouement,* and these are flanked by an *introduction* and a *conclusion.*

The concentric development shows the limits of the

various parts quite well in most cases. In Mark the *narration* runs from the withdrawal of John the Baptist after Jesus' baptism to the account of his death (1:14—6:13); the argumentation runs from the feeding of the 5,000 to the cure of the blind man at Jericho (6:30—10:52), and the denouement from the arrival at Jerusalem to the death on the cross (11:1—15:47).

The Prologue

At this point we shall consider only the first and the last parts. What functions do they have in a drama or discourse and to what extent is this verified in Mark?[3] The *introduction* (prologue) of a discourse should give the tone, establish contact with the hearers, and announce the subject. Some emotion may be introduced, to the extent that the hearers are appealed to directly. More care was devoted to the *introduction* than perhaps any other part of the discourse, especially to the very first words which break the silence.

The *conclusion* (epilogue) is the closure and dismissal. The orator should sum up what he wanted to say and take leave of his hearers, not without an appeal to them for one last time and good and all. In general a *short* conclusion was preferred; the orator must avoid starting over in summing up. Often emotion was not lacking.

Mark's *introduction* brings Jesus, the protagonist, on the scene, first through an intermediary, John the Baptist, who points him out. The second pericope, the baptism scene, continues to reveal Jesus to us, especially by the voice from heaven which expresses his complete identity: "Thou art my beloved Son; with thee I am well pleased," (1:11). The third unit of the *introduction* (1:12-13) transmits the last information to the readers: the Son of God, full of the Holy Spirit, was led into the wilderness, there to be tested by Satan. These two verses reveal completely the

[3]*Ibid.,* pp. 83-106.

depth of the drama getting under way.

In drama this first part was traditionally called the *prologue*. In the Hellenistic age the word did not mean solely a prelude or introduction to the action; it also designated an actor, the first to appear on the scene. This actor plays the role of a messenger (*aggelos*), often a messenger from a god, and his monologue introduces the spectators to the action. Often he does not take part in the main action but disappears once and for all at the end of the *introduction*. Sometimes this messenger is the spokesman for the author and addresses the audience in his name. He may communicate information that he alone knows— natural enough in the case of a god's messenger—while one or the other, or all the characters in the drama, continue in ignorance until the *recognition*. In these cases the difference of points of view between the spectators and the characters of the drama is essential for the understanding of the denouement of the action and for the perception of its effects.

The role of John the Baptist at the beginning of Mark's gospel corresponds in a striking way to that of the *prologue* in a Hellenistic drama. The first personage on the scene, he introduces the protagonist, exhorts the audience to prepare for the coming of the one whom he announces, and disappears as soon as the protagonist has appeared on the scene.

The Epilogue

Jesus dies on the cross, is taken down and placed in the tomb, and the stone is rolled to the door. But there is an *epilogue*. The women go to anoint the body of the crucified (16:1), but their initiative is anticipated by another who intervenes and surprises them. The account is full of surprises. The women set out very early in the morning, yet, behold, "the sun had already risen," (16:2). They are worried about the stone ("Who will roll away the stone for us from the door of the tomb?" vs. 3) and behold the stone was rolled back. "It was very large," the narrator adds, suggesting the marvelous, superhuman character of the operation. They enter the tomb and even before they can take note of the absence of the body, "they saw a young man sitting on the right side, dressed in a white robe," (vs. 5). His message continues in the same vein of marvelous anticipation. "Jesus has risen," he says, even before indicating that "he is not here"; he "is going before" the disciples to Galilee; there they will see him "as he told you," (vs. 7). The women are overcome by trembling and astonishment, "and they said nothing to anyone, for they were afraid," (vs. 8).

This finale is a dramatic counterpoint to the denouement of the action, the death and burial of the protagonist. Now the question is, to what extent does this finale correspond to a traditional dramatic *epilogue*?

The principal personage of this last pericope of the gospel is the "young man" who appears in the tomb, substituting himself for the body placed there by Joseph of Arimathea (15:45-46; 16:5). His role is that of a messenger, and in this role he is comparable to that of the *aggelos* of ancient tragedy. The function of these messengers was to report what the ancients considered too marvelous or too cruel to be represented on the stage. The objective of drama, Aristotle had written, is not to horrify but to provoke the pleasure (*hedone*) of a strong emotion of fear or of pity. The "young man's" message is concerned with events calculated to evoke just such fear and awe as Aristotle had spoken of: a resurrection from the dead and appearance of the Risen Jesus.

Deus ex Machina

The intervention of the "young man" resembles the traditional *coup de theatre* called *deus ex machina*, the descent of a god or some divine personage by *machina*. "Tragedy sometimes uses a crane to bring deities and heroes flying through the air; the actor would in such a case be suspended on a rope and swung into our view by the crane, which would be mounted on the top rear of the *skene*."⁴ This personage untangles the drama, often when it has arrived at its most inextricable point. He often reveals the future, the consequences of the tragic crisis, and by his divine authority provokes a conversion of the personage to whom he appears, lifting their hearts to a new level.

In ancient dramatic composition the messenger scene does not necessarily appear in the epilogue, but from the time of Euripides there was a tendency to place the messenger scene in the epilogue and to make it correspond with the introduction, the prologue. Likewise in Mark there is a parallel between the role of John the Baptist in the prologue —and there he is designated by the term *aggelos* (vs. 2)— and that of the "young man" in the epilogue (*neaniskos* and *aggelos* were synonyms). The first announces the coming of Jesus, but effaces himself as soon as the one he has announced appears; the latter substitutes for the risen one of whom he is also the herald. Both remain outside the main action. Both are bearers of a message—*euanggelion*—which is addressed in the first place to the characters in the drama: the crowd, from all parts, comes for John the Baptist, and the few women, whose names are given, for the "young man." But these two audiences do not have a strict connection with the action, or with the characters in the narrative, so the communication is really addressed to the readers of the gospel. This was one of the functions of the prologue and epilogue, to establish contact with the spectators at the beginning and to take leave of them at the end.

The Women's Fear

Finally the gospel ends on a note of fear. At least four terms refer to this final sentiment: "they were amazed,"

---

⁴K. J. Dover, *Aristophanic Comedy*, (Berkeley: University of California Press, 1972), pp. 25-26.

(vss. 5,6); "trembling and astonishment," (vs. 8a); "for they were afraid" (vs. 8c). This sentiment is entirely appropriate for a tragedy: Aristotle teaches throughout his treatise *Poetics* that fear and pity are the emotions which all tragic poetry seeks to elicit. In Mark the fear and the final silence are recounted. The drama is embedded in the narrative: the narrative recounts the very effects of the dramatic action. We note further that the mention of the women's silence in the finale has a corresponding element at the beginning of the gospel: the text begins with the formal statement, "The beginning of the good news." At the end of the account, all is silence, leaving only a religious fear, underlining the words of the messenger.

Therefore the epilogue of Mark's gospel has several characteristics in common with the conventional finale of a Hellenistic drama. And we found the same to be true of the prologue. Prologue and epilogue tie the whole of Mark's gospel together in a concentric development. And the same is true of parts within the gospel. Furthermore, at the juncture points we find *transition passages*, low-key anecdotes somewhat in the nature of digressions, which serve as bridges between two parts, repeating elements from the passage just completed, and anticipating elements from the passage just ahead. Standaert lists eight such passages: among them, the martyrdom of John the Baptist, the poor widow in the temple, the young man fleeing naked, the young man in the tomb.

Thus there are many points in the composition of Mark where we believe we can see the influence of contemporary dramatic art in its conventional forms. One could doubt such an impact if this influence had been noticeable only in a single place in the gospel account. "The fact that it can be seen at the key junctures of the articulation of the narrative makes this influence almost certain."[5]

---

[5]Standaert, p. 104.

CHAPTER 7

RESURRECTION RECALLED AS MYSTERY AND WONDER

IT HAS BEEN ARGUED by some that Mark's gospel has no other purpose than that which supposedly every gospel must have—to preserve the traditions necessary for the upbuilding of the church. But Mark is such a subtle and complex work that the author's purpose clearly involves more than just preserving traditions. And as to traditions, Mark probably did not have a completely free hand in dealing with these. Not only the smallest units of tradition but also more inclusive complexes of tradition must have been available to him in fairly fixed form. The general framework would have been provided by the pattern used in kerygmatic summaries of the message concerning Jesus and those events which were connected with his name, from the baptism of John up to the resurrection.[1]

It has been suggested that the difficulties St. Paul experienced at Corinth illustrate the problems associated with having traditions about Jesus in small units, without a controlling context. Paul told stories about Jesus and

---

[1]Cf., N. Dahl, *Jesus in the Memory of the Early Church*, (Minneapolis: Augsburg, 1976), p. 52.

quoted sayings of Jesus. Knowing that the Eucharist celebrated events leading up to Jesus' resurrection, Paul's converts got so carried away that their celebration of this joyful event became unseemly. Stories told about Jesus apart from a controlling context were open to misunderstanding.

Mark seems to have been the inventor of the gospel form. It was he who hit on the idea of collecting the traditions about Jesus into a narrative whose order and arrangement itself would provide, with a minimum of editorial comment, the context for understanding and interpreting those traditions. Rather than interlace incident with comment on the way the incident was to be understood, Mark chose to let the traditions speak for themselves. The interpretative context was to be the key, not the author's own theological expositions. Thus the traditions remain free to make their original points, but the way they are arranged and juxtaposed provides the clue as to the overall context within which those points are to be understood.

Beginning and End

Mark's unusual beginning and ending exemplify how much can be said by arrangement and context, without explicit, direct comment. Unlike Matthew and Luke, Mark has no infancy narrative. He plunges into the middle of things, with the appearance of John the Baptist and Jesus' baptism.

In just thirteen verses Mark manages to make an affirmation about who Jesus is by a deft use of basic biblical concepts. The Old Testament is written forwards and backwards from the Exodus. Mark evokes the new, definitive Exodus in his description of the New Israel, passing through the water and then withdrawing into the desert place for testing. Jesus' appearance is preceded by that of the eschatological prophet who affirms that not he but Jesus is the Messiah. The Spirit hovers over the water as at the first creation, and a voice from heaven identifies

Jesus with the Suffering Servant. Mark expects a lot of his readers.

The end of the gospel is even stranger—so strange that commentators have often refused to accept the fact that the gospel ends where it apparently does, and they have undertaken to supply the missing ending. In his last chapter Mark relates that three women went to Jesus' tomb, found the stone rolled back, and, inside, a young man in a white robe. "And they were amazed (*ekthambeo*). And he said to them, 'Do not be amazed (*ekthambeo*)'" (vss. 5-6). The young man tells the women to go and tell Jesus' disciples and Peter that he was going before them to Galilee. And the woman "went out and fled from the tomb; for trembling (*tromos*) and astonishment (*ekstasis*) had come upon them; and they said nothing to any one, for they were afraid (*ephobounto gar*)," (vs. 8).

"They were afraid . . ."

Even to this day some commentators have refused to accept this as the original ending of Mark's gospel. They argue: a sentence, still less a book, cannot end with *gar*; the verb "to fear (*phobeomai*)" requires a conclusion; we must be shown that the women's fear was dispelled and their silence and disobedience resolved; and above all they argue that one or more of the manifestations of the Risen Lord must be narrated, so that the book ends on a note of victory and happiness.

The argument based on the use of *gar* has been shown to be invalid. Numerous precedents have established that sentences and even paragraphs can end with the word *gar* ("for") and that a two-word sentence has to end with *gar*. A recent theory would have it that both the beginning and the ending of Mark's gospel are missing. It is argued that the change from scroll to codex came not later than A.D. 130 and may have begun to take place as early as A.D. 70. If one end of a scroll is damaged, there is no reason why the other end should be damaged also. But if the last leaf of a codex has been torn off, there is at least a possibility that the first leaf also will have disappeared.

The greatest difficulty for the theory of the lost pages is the fact that the manuscript evidence is strongly against it. The long ending(s), 16:9-20, is omitted by the two most ancient Greek uncial manuscripts of the New Testament, Codex Vaticanus and Codex Sinaiticus, both of the fourth century. The long ending is a concise statement of the appearances of Jesus, his final command to the disciples, his ascension, and the preaching of the gospel throughout the whole world. It was composed by borrowing elements from the other gospels and appended to Mark, probably between A.D. 100 and 140. Since it can be shown that Mark's gospel without the long ending tells an intelligible and consistent story, the long ending should be abandoned. Indeed, it is only in this form that Mark's gospel does tell an intelligible and consistent story.

Fear and Awe

Supporters of the longer ending have also argued that it is unacceptable that a gospel should end on a note of fear; that we must be shown that the women's fear was dispelled and their silence and disobedience resolved. But, as we have seen, fear and awe are the proper outcome of a drama, and we must note what kind of fear Mark has in mind. The authors of the long ending to Mark seem to presuppose that the women's silence was due to a fear of men, while the whole tenor of 16:1-8 shows the amazement, flight, trembling, astonishment, and finally fear on the part of the women to have been due to fear or dread of God, to fear caused by revelation, and not to fear of men. The women had received a command, but owing to the unnerving effect which it had upon them they were unable to obey it.

Reverential fear in the face of revelation runs like a thread all through the gospel, appearing also as amazement and astonishment. When Jesus came down from the mount of Transfiguration, Mark writes that all the crowd "were greatly amazed" (*ekthambeo*, 9:15), the same word that is used of the women at the tomb. After Jesus calmed the wind and the sea for the first time and rebuked the disciples for their lack of faith, "they were filled with awe (*phobeomai*) and said to one another, 'Who then is this, that even the wind and the sea obey him?'" (4:41). The silence of the women at the tomb and the inarticulate, bewildered utterance of the disciples in this latter instance are of the same nature and they arise from the same cause, namely, an increasing and involuntary realization of the nature and being of Him with whom they have to do.

The women's fear is not dispelled and their silence and disobedience are not resolved, for the same reason that the narrator deliberately creates a narrative world in which the incomprehension of the disciples is never dispelled. Those are necessary elements in any valid description of what life beyond the empty tomb is like. If the reader brings in elements from the other gospels, Mark's arrangement is rendered ineffective.

While fear is a theme that runs all through the gospel, it is one of those elements whose function shifts as we move from the first to the second part of the gospel and which therefore imparts structure to the gospel. Fear is the normal result of divine revelation. Fear is mentioned in connection with the first stilling of the storm (4:35-41); Gerasene demoniac (5:1-20); Transfiguration (9:2-8); tomb (16:1-8). Astonishment is mentioned in connection with the Capernaum demoniac (1:21-28); deaf and dumb man (7:31-37); raising the daughter of Jairus (5:35-43). For Mark the first and inevitable result of the realization of men of the presence of revelation is fear or astonishment, or both. But this fear and astonishment is by no means the purpose of the revelation, and in themselves they are undesirable. They result from want of faith and understanding (6:50-52; 8:21).

Religious Fear

The response to Jesus' mighty words and works on the part of the crowds and disciples is religious fear, wonderment, amazement; the response of the enemies is murderous hatred. There are two groups in the gospel who do not respond to Jesus' words and works with religious fear and wonder, viz., the demons and the enemies. Even Herod's fear of John the Baptist seems to possess a religious strain, and Pilate's amazement might be construed as religious. As Aloysius Ambrozic wrote: "No matter how reprehensible Mark may consider fear and amazement to be, he obviously looks upon it as a glimmer of conversion, faith, and understanding. The enemies of Jesus, however, are never taught and never respond with religious amazement."[2]

Most of Jesus' miracles come before Caesarea Philippi and these are what cause the fear and astonishment, rather than the teaching. Only the demons acknowledge Jesus' messiahship during this time, while his enemies clearly detect something ominous in his words and deeds. At Caesarea Philippi Peter acknowledges Jesus' messiahship. But when Jesus begins to predict his passion, it becomes evident that Peter's concept of messiahship is so defective that his is no acknowledgement at all and Jesus puts him on the same footing as the demons. After Caesarea Philippi it is not Jesus' messianic acts that cause fear and astonishment. From Caesarea Philippi to the end of the book it is Jesus' teaching that causes amazement, astonishment, and fear.

The reaction of the women at the tomb, then, their amazement, trembling, astonishment, and fear, gathers up the emotions caused, throughout the book, first by the Lord's messianic actions and secondly by his teaching on the meaning of those messianic actions. In 16:1-8 the women are faced by the fact of the empty tomb and the instructions the "young man" gives them. Owing to their imperfect

[2] *The Hidden Kingdom*, (Washington: Catholic Biblical Association, 1972), Monograph Series II, p. 59.

faith, their lack of insight and understanding, the result is inevitable and their reaction is in full accord with all that Mark has taught us in these matters earlier in his gospel. The women's actions also serve to transfer the mystery and ambiguity which surrounded the disciples throughout the narrative into the reader's time. Even in the time beyond the empty tomb the reader is confronted by the same challenge to faith.

No Resurrection Appearances

Supporters of the long ending also argue that Mark's gospel should end with a resurrection appearance and a description of Jesus' reunion with his disciples in Galilee, a twice-promised reunion (14:28; 16:7). Mark describes neither of them, but quite simply takes them for granted. Mark assumes throughout that his readers are acquainted with the root-facts of the Christian religion; the way in which Jesus is brought upon the scene at his baptism would alone be sufficient evidence of this. The inevitable conclusion is that Mark is "writing for believers who already knew the facts of the Gospel, and, still more important, had day by day in themselves and in the evidence of the progress of the Gospel the witness of the power which the manifestation of the risen Lord first infused into disciples."[3]

Mark's account points beyond itself; the gospel presupposes that the silence of the women was not the last of the Easter events. In his Farewell Discourse Jesus foresees a time when the disciples' incomprehension will come to an end; Peter will give up his error and it will become the error of others. During the time before the end, the gospel is to be proclaimed to all nations (13:10; 14:9), and what remained hidden during Jesus' earthly life will be preached in public (9:9). The words "tell the disciples and Peter" (16:7) hint at appearances and the whole gospel points

[3]R. H. Lightfoot, *Gospel Message*, p. 95.

forward to a decisive turning point when this happens.

That Mark mentions neither the fact nor the manner of the resurrection appearances does not mean that he intended to veil the secret. It means rather that his readers were already informed; Mark presupposes the readers' knowledge of the events subsequent to the women's flight from the empty tomb. In other words, the book is intended for Christian readers who have already had the good news of Jesus' resurrection proclaimed to them and who have believed, at one time at least, if only imperfectly. The written gospel points beyond itself to the living word in the church, that message which the disciples were commissioned to proclaim when the risen Christ appeared to them. As Nils Dahl puts it: "The goal is not to awaken faith but to recall the character of the resurrection as a mystery and wonder which could elicit fear and awe. The conclusion suggests that the evangelist did not intend to write an 'aid for mission work,' but writes for believers and wants to clarify for them what faith and the Gospel really involve."[4]

Messianic Secret

Since the turn of the century Mark's gospel has been identified with the idea of a "messianic secret." Taking his lead from a number of passages where Jesus works some messianic act and then commands the witnesses to remain silent about it, Wilhelm Wrede argued that Mark worked this element into his gospel to solve a Christological problem troubling the Church of his time. Wrede claimed that the messianic secret was an attempt to harmonize the earlier view that Jesus became the Messiah only at the resurrection with the later view that Jesus' earthly life had a messianic character. More widespread than Wrede's own explanation of the messianic secret is the view that it is apologetic in character: that the injunctions to silence and the theme of hardening of hearts explain Jesus' rejection

---

[4]*Jesus in the Memory*, p. 55.

by his own people though he was the Messiah and a great worker of miracles.

Actually the reader of Mark is in on the "messianic secret" from the beginning: he is told that Jesus is the Messiah in 1:1. The so-called messianic secret is better called the "Christ mystery" and is by no means limited to the question of Jesus' messiahship. "Mark is not presenting the solution to something which has been an unanswered riddle; he is emphasizing the mysterious character of something with which his readers are familiar."[5]

Anamnesis

Mark is writing for those already in the church who have received the secret of God's kingdom as a gift. His goal is to remind them of what is contained in the secret, so that they may understand what has been given to them. Mark's purpose is not kerygmatic in the sense of proclamation but in the sense of recollection (*anamnesis*), a restoring to memory.

The Easter events place a dividing line between the period of Jesus the hidden Messiah and Jesus openly proclaimed as the Crucified and Risen One. But this does not mean that the possibility for failure among Jesus' followers has ceased. Mark's conclusion shows on the contrary that even when the message that Jesus is risen is proclaimed by angels, those who hear can react in a manner which is no more adequate than that of the disciples when Jesus was among them. The members of the Church who have partaken of the full revelation must see to it that they do not fail as the disciples did before them. The superimposition of the two time frames is so handled that the reader is confronted by the same challenge to faith as were Jesus' contemporaries.

Mark is not writing with a missionary aim but wants those who already believe, even if imperfectly, to under-

[5]*Ibid.*, p. 56.

stand the proper significance of the Gospel. "He reminds them that the Christ in whom they believe is the one who lived as the hidden Son of man and died as the rejected Messiah. The emphasis on those points in the narrative which evoke fear and astonishment is a cry to awaken, addressed to a church in danger of taking the Gospel for granted. This call to faith, to endurance in affliction, and to watchfulness is combined with a warning against self-assurance and ambitious strivings."[6]

---

[6]*Ibid.*, p. 64.

CHAPTER 8
KERYGMA AND DIDACHE
IN MARK

THREE PRINCIPAL PHASES can often be discerned in the classical Greek drama: complication, crisis (identification), and denouement. Mark's gospel too has a recognition scene at its middle. It divides into two parts at 8:27-30, Peter's confession at Caesarea Philippi, and there are notable differences between the two parts.

In his 1967 thesis *The Mind of Mark*, Quentin Quesnell undertook a thoroughgoing analysis of Mark's two-fold structure. Taking the division at 8:27 as his starting point, Quesnell examines the change after 8:27 under a number of headings. Among the changes of *vocabulary* and *style* are: references to "bread" cease; explicit references to the non-understanding of the disciples cease (though the theme continues in a new form); the amount of space given to words of Jesus rises. Changes in the presentation of the *figure* of Christ can be detected. Mark begins to present Christ as a figure of destiny whose fate is entirely marked out for him, beginning with the first "the Son of Man *must* (*dei*) suffer" in 8:31. It is emphasized that this fate is determined by Scripture. And this destiny becomes the basis of exhortation to the disciples. "If anyone wants to come after me, let him take up his cross." By way of contrast, if the gospel of Mark had stopped at 8:26, Jesus would be a great prophet, teacher, healer, but he would not have been the Crucified Messiah.

Other lesser changes include: the appearance of a new set of adversaries—"the chief priests, scribes, and elders;" the apostles begin to speak as individuals for the first time in the gospel; and the first references to the Father appear.

Moral Directives

Perhaps the most significant difference after 8:27 is the extraordinary extent to which Jesus' *universal moral directives* have been gathered into this one part of the gospel. Moral directives beginning "Whoever would . . ." appear nine times, while none appear clearly in the first part. Such moral directives phrased in other ways (conditionally, negatively, etc.) occur some twenty times. "Clearly, the entire gospel is concerned somehow with moral questions. But just as clearly, the universal moral exhortations, directives, and—in general—positive teachings have all been gathered into the second half of the gospel, especially into 8,27 to 10,45."[1]

What can we conclude from these observations? Quesnell's conclusion is that there is only one explanation which will account for all of these simultaneously: these are redactional phenomena. For his own reasons Mark has concentrated the moral teaching into this one part of the gospel. Here he begins the open discussion of the destiny which awaits Jesus, brings into play certain ways of phrasing things and certain characteristic actions on the part of his principal characters, and moves to a new stage in the discussion of Jesus' identity.

And what are the consequences as far as the first half of the gospel is concerned? It is equally important to notice

[1]Quentin Quesnell, S.J., *The Mind of Mark*, (Rome: Pontifical Biblical Institute, 1969), pp. 147-48.

that if the author is redacting when he gathers all that
material into the section after 8:27, then he was redacting
equally in all the earlier parts of the gospel, where he
avoided recording that material. When Jesus "teaches" or
"speaks the word" in the first half, those were all occasions
when he could have spoken at length on any of the themes
which in fact Mark reserves for 8:27 and following.

Mark was thinking of the second half of his gospel when
he redacted the first half; redacting the first part he had in
mind a plan which called for reserving certain material for
the second half. He planned that Jesus should reveal himself
at the proper time as predestined Son of Man, that at that
same time he should begin in concentrated fashion to give
universal moral directives to his disciples, directives which
are often directly dependent on the destiny Jesus would
describe for himself—suffering, cross, loss of life, and
return in glory.

Mark the Redactor

Mark could not achieve this effect without changing
the tradition he was working with. As was mentioned
earlier, Mark did not have a completely free hand in dealing
with tradition. Not only small units of tradition but also
more inclusive complexes of tradition were available to him
in a fairly fixed form. The general framework was provided
by a pattern used in kerygmatic summaries of the message
concerning Jesus and those events which were connected
with his name, from the baptism by John up to the resurrection. Summaries of the kerygma are found in the Acts of the
Apostles and in the epistles. This kerygma was a dominating
and coordinating factor in the gathering and ordering of
separate gospel traditions. From the beginning the kerygma
and gospel tradition were interwoven and dependent on
each other. The early church's preaching and teaching not
only built on the relatively independent pericopes of the
words of Jesus and stories from his life, but also on "a
complete picture of the person and life of Jesus, which had

a firm basis in the belief of the community. This belief, furthermore, was grounded in previous historical events which were experienced and witnessed by people who still lived and acted as tradition bearers at the time when the Gospel tradition—at least the synoptic Gospel tradition—received its final written form."[2]

Mark's presentation of the life of Jesus up to the beginning of the passion corresponds quite closely to the order of events as given in the kerygma. However, besides this arrangement there runs another basic plan in the gospel of Mark, a plan of systematic or christological type which shows a clear transition between 8:26 and 8:27. Riesenfeld characterizes the first main part under the heading "the Son of Man and Israel" (ministry of Jesus among the people and the opposition raised). The other main part, which runs up to 13:37, may be said to deal with the subject "the Messiah as teacher and prophet."

Proclamation and Teaching

This latter arrangement bears undeniable features of theological, christological reflection. The christological has been superimposed on the historically stylized arrangement. Mighty works and proclamation (*kerygma*) stand in the foreground in the first part, while teaching (*didache*) predominates in the second (passion predictions and teaching on discipleship). The same sequence is found in the epistles. However, there are signs which indicate that the characteristic concentration of teaching (*didache*), mainly intended for the education of the disciples, was not found in the original tradition material but is the result of Mark's editorial activity. Thus the picture of Jesus, as first publicly active in Galilee preaching and performing miracles and thereafter limiting his activity more or less to the circle of disciples, was not part of the original tradition, but resulted from Mark's editorial activity.

[2]Harald Riesenfeld, *The Gospel Tradition*, (Philadelphia: Fortress Press, 1970), p. 54.

If the concentration of teaching were strictly historical the term "teach" (*didasko*) should be found mainly in the second part. In actual fact *"teach"* (*didasko*) and "proclaim" (*kerusso*) appear side by side in the first part. What can we conclude from these circumstances: the occurrence of *didasko* also in the first half of the gospel, and the concentration of the teaching in the second part?

"Without doubt," Riesenfeld asserts, "it was necessitated by the church's position at the time of the editing of the material. As Christian teaching had been systematized and consolidated during the first decades of the early church, something we know thanks to the New Testament epistles, it was felt suitable to bring together the teaching material in the tradition about Jesus to show that 'the doctrine' of the Christian life had its origin in the actual teaching of Jesus. The disciples thus become prototypes for Christians who are led into the way of discipleship."[3]

Mark's description of Jesus' ministry in two parts has its equivalent in actual fact in the twofold nature of the missionary message of the early church. This message was also kerygmatic in that its essence was the message about Jesus Christ, his earthly life, passion, death, and resurrection. But there is an important difference between the kerygma of God's kingdom proclaimed by Jesus and the Christ kerygma of the early church. The latter assumes the events of Easter as historical fact. As a consequence, the former part of Mark's gospel and the early Christian missionary message correspond to each other only schematically or in principle. But the case is not the same regarding the part dealing with discipleship and the teaching of the early church. Here there are striking similarities. Here Mark seems to have been influenced by the practice of the church he knew when selecting and forming the traditional material.

[3]*Ibid.*, pp. 65-66.

Gateway to Discipleship

The incident which begins the second part, Peter's confession at Caesarea Philippi, forms the introduction to the whole of the passage in Mark which contains the didactic material. Mark understood the disciple's confession of Jesus as Messiah as the gateway leading into true discipleship, the path of teaching and initiation. Peter's confession here becomes the prerequisite for Jesus to disclose the core of his teachings about the mission of the Son of Man and the demands of discipleship.

When we think of the historical course of events, it is naturally an anomaly that the missionary task of the twelve disciples in Galilee occurs prior to Jesus' teaching about the fundamental things of the new life. On the other hand, it is quite the contrary if we think about the position of the church after Easter and Pentecost. There the kerygmatic call leads to confession of faith and baptism, after which teaching, instruction on living the Christian life, may begin within the framework of the community.

It is natural then that Jesus' miracles are chiefly found in the first part of the gospel, since they belong to the kerygmatic preaching of Jesus. Why then do miracles also appear in the second part? Does this not break down the structure we have delineated? A closer examination of the miracles in question provides an answer. As the story of the epileptic boy (9:14-29) is presented, it has the form of a pronouncement story; that is, an episode which terminates in a saying of Jesus. "The point is, therefore, not the miracle itself or the confession of faith made by the father of the sick boy, but rather the attitude of Jesus to the problem of the disciples' incapacity to perform mighty works."[4]

By adopting the procedure just outlined Mark is able to present Jesus' teaching in a particular context and the results are very effective. Jesus' teaching on discipleship is presented in the context of the journey to Jerusalem and in

[4]*Ibid.*, pp. 72-73.

close conjunction with the three passion predictions. And our use of the historical method seems justified in this instance because the redactional pattern is sufficiently broad to be manageable. It is a different matter when a text is split down into a multitude of fragments.

CHAPTER 9
JESUS' POWERFUL ACTS

MARK'S FIRST VERSE makes an identification: Jesus is "Christ, the Son of God." The reader knows who Jesus is from the beginning, while this knowledge is hidden from the people involved in the action. This sets up a situation of dramatic irony, which usually depends on the characters of the play being ignorant of significant knowledge that is available to the spectator-reader. The prologue ends with Jesus' experience in the wilderness. After that, Mark rapidly sketches the beginning of Jesus' public ministry: Jesus proclaims the presence of the Kingdom, calls disciples, works miracles.

From the prologue on, the narrative is pared down to a fast moving sequence of activity. One way that Mark achieves this is to reduce the notations of time and place to a minimum. Apart from the general movement of the story from Galilee to Jerusalem, the gospel exhibits little geographical or temporal structure or specificity. Mark introduces individual incidents with general terms such as "one sabbath" (2:23) or "again" (3:1, 20; 4:1). Scenes are set "beside the sea" or "in the synagogue."

One element in the clipped, racy style is parataxis—ranging sentences one after another with no other connection than *kai* ("and") when the use of subordinate clauses would be expected. Paratactic expression is one element that distinguishes oral discourse from written composition.

The unsophisticated ear is far less sensitive to parataxis than the erudite reader's eye. "If most of the Gospel was originally a transcript from oral sources, it is understandable that it contains this type of sentence structure. If the Gospel was destined for public reading rather than private study, it is even more understandable."[1] There are other means than the spoken word to express the relation of thought to thought. Looks and gestures can sometimes express far more than bare words.

A Narrator's Art

Indeed, expressive looks and gestures have been incorporated into the text itself. The gospel abounds in picturesque details and lifelike suggestions: an expressive gesture or impressive look caught by Mark's pen, or a mood described by a relevant verb, or details of setting given in passing. In the synagogue at Capernaum, Jesus rebukes the unclean spirit, saying, "Be silent and come out of him!" (1:25). When some criticize Jesus for curing the man with the withered hand, "he looked around at them with anger and grieved at their hardness of heart," (3:5). Jesus looks up to heaven and sighs (7:34); he sees the throng and has compassion (6:34); he marvels at unbelief (6:6); Jesus rebukes Peter (8:33) and is indignant when the children are denied admittance to him (10:14). Matthew too speaks of Jesus' putting a child in the midst of the disciples but Mark adds that Jesus "took him in his arms" (9:36); in the first storm Jesus is "in the stern, asleep on the cushion," (4:38), and when he is awakened he "rebuked the wind and said to the sea, 'Peace! Be still!'"

Especially striking is the fact that these features do not seem to result from strenuous efforts to produce a work of high literary quality; they appear suddenly and almost naturally, as if brought in by the narration itself. They reveal the art not of a story writer but of a narrator, a person who is interested primarily in recounting the most

[1]Bilezikian, *op. cit.*, p. 115.

important facts, but who, in the course of his discourse, can stress a point with a motion, a silence, or an expressive look. These effects, proper to oral delivery, were apparently integrated into the gospel so that they could be renewed with each public reading.

This quality of Mark's gospel was fully recognized and exploited by Alec McCowen in his solo performance. As Dr. Janet Larson wrote of it: "McCowen's deliberate repetition of significant gestures, of facial changes, of shifts in tone, and of certain blocking patterns brings vividly before our attention Mark's thematic design. McCowen's portrayal makes even more persuasive the patterning that dominates Mark 8-10, picking up echoes all over this Gospel: Jesus' prescience about his fate, the disciples' lack of comprehension, their master's corrective teaching about discipleship, and miraculous confirmation. In McCowen's enactment these rhythms are unmistakably felt."[2]

McCowen's Greatest Script

Seasoned by thirty-five years of stage, film and television experience, McCowen looked at the Synoptics for material suited to a one-man show, and he found that, unlike Matthew and Luke, Mark spoke to him in "wonderful theatrical terms." In this discovery his actor's instinct was unerring and he determined to perform the gospel as a complete, unedited script. "This was the greatest script I had ever found."

McCowen's performance alone challenges the view that Mark was an inept writer—patching episodes together every which way. The narrative is performed in such a way that we are made aware of the juxtaposed motifs, we experience their thematic aptness and thus their persuasive power. Mark's notorious awkwardness in chronology and geography present no problem: time transitions are not

[2]"St. Alec's Gospel," *The Christian Century*, 96:1, 17.

always needed and uncertainty about Jesus' whereabouts is conjured away by the creation of theatrical space as McCowen moves about the stage.

The performance makes it clear that Mark's work is dramatic .The language is not at all the diction of a historian but that of a narrator. Primarily, however, the drama of proclamation in Mark is enacted by deeds rather than by words. Mark's notion of gospel is itself profoundly dramatic —the good news in God's saving acts through the career and person of Jesus Christ. Mark's practice of bracketing one tradition by two halves of another creates sharp theatrical pleasure by embedding stories within stories.

"Because the Jesus traditions upon which Mark drew contained forms refined by oral transmission, it is not surprising that they held up well in dramatic performance— the scenes, the memorable vignettes and anecdotes, often rounded off with a generalizing conclusion."[3] Many such rounded-off stories evoke aesthetic pleasure not only because of their sense of closure, but also because they turn upon a verbal or dramatic reversal. And the presence of these closures raises a question regarding 16:8. Is it a competent closure, even if rightly interpreted (see Chapter 24)?

Powerful Acts

In the first phase of Mark's gospel, the complication, the miracles are the key element. Almost half of the first ten chapters is given over, directly or indirectly, to miracle stories, and they extend into the second half as well. Regarding these it should first be said that the makers of the gospel traditions held unanimously the biblical view of the nature of God. He is the living God, personal and active, known more through what he does than in his being. God is conceived of as Power, and there are no limitations to God's power. Yet, because he is moral and holy, he is not

---

[3]*Ibid.*, p. 18.

capricious. The Lord God intervenes in history to save his people, he leads them out of Egypt by the strength of his hand (Ex 13:9) and he uses nature to achieve his purpose, sending a strong east wind to divide the waters (14:21).

This view of God's nature carries over into the New Testament, so much so that power (*dunamis*) is even used as a synonym for God. Asked at his trial before Caiaphas if he was the Messiah, Jesus replied: "I am; and you will see the Son of Man seated at the right hand of power," (14:62). *Exousia*, "liberty of action, authority" is practically a synonym of *dunamis*. It is also clear that the New Testament, like the Old Testament, believes that ordinarily God's power is veiled, hidden. It is seen only in his acts of revelation.

Jesus' powerful acts are momentary manifestations that God's power is working in and through him. The early christian community seems to have regarded Jesus' powerful acts "in a twofold light: as a manifestation of the power of God active in Jesus, a proclamation of the fullness of time (cf. 1:15), and as signs of the redemption which Jesus had wrought, as prophetic signs."[4] Jesus' power over the fever of Simon's mother-in-law, which yielded to his imperious gesture, proclaims that the reign of God is a present reality. And the words, "he raised her up," had a special symbolic meaning in a catechetical milieu. Jesus is the Saviour who by the deeds of his earthly life has prefigured the realities of the divine life now communicated to believers. At the same time, we need to recall that miracles are muted signs, open to different interpretations. Even in their presence, God's veiledness is not dissipated.

The New Testament does not use Jesus' miracles to give us an insight into his psychology; its does not present them as either motivated or unmotivated.

For some the miracles are evidence of Jesus' compassion, but little is said in the gospels about this matter. Of the synoptics, Matthew alone exhibits a tendency

---

[4]Wilfrid Harrington, *Mark*, (Wilmington: Michael Glazier, Inc., 1979), p. 19.

attention to the compassion of Jesus, but even here the tendency is not strong. The gospel writers "lived in an age unaffected by the humanistic approach and the humanitarian attitude which are the results of the rise of European liberalism, itself doubtless on its ethical side a product of the Christian conscience which the Church has bred within western civilization."[5]

For their part the form critics proceeded from the preconceived principle that miracles are impossible and sought the origin of miracle or wonder stories in other circumstances than in the historical career of Jesus. Judaism attributed marvelous deeds to Palestinian rabbis and the Hellenistic world attributed them to professional wonder-workers. The general thesis of form criticism is that Christianity could not have converted a world, whether Jewish or Gentile, that gave credence to such miracles unless Jesus was presented as an equal, at least, in miraculous power. And so miracle narratives were supposedly invented for Jesus.

No Compelling Proof

But one thing does emerge clearly from the comparison of the gospel miracle stories with pagan and Jewish miracle stories. It tells us something about the evidential value of miracles—what miracles could and could not prove. In New Testament times the ability to work miracles was not in itself regarded as proof of divinity. The ability was ascribed to both Jews and pagans, as well as the followers of Jesus. This circumstance has an important bearing on the Christ mystery in Mark. The question as to Jesus' nature and role was not dispelled solely by the fact that he worked miracles.

The miracles were not compelling proofs. As C.E.B. Cranfield writes in his commentary on Mark: "Their true significance is recognizable only by faith. They are, as it

[5]Alan Richardson, *The Miracle Stories of the Gospels*, (London: SCM Press, 1941), p. 32.

were, chinks in the curtain of the Son of God's hiddenness. The light let through the chinks is real light (the miracles do reveal, they are an effective manifestation of Christ's glory for those who believe (cf. Jn 2:11), and failure to discern their meaning and to respond to the summons to repentance which they constitute is without excuse...but the light is not so direct as to be compelling."[6]

There are several reasons why it is not. Other people were credited with miracles; the amazement which the miracles cause is offset by the apparent weakness and unimpressiveness of him who works them; there were striking external similarities between many of Jesus' healing miracles and those attributed to others. Thus other explanations lay close to hand besides that advanced by the Christian believer: another prophet, another rabbi, or even just another wonder-worker. The miracles are not inconsistent with the general veiledness or indirectness of God's self-disclosure in Jesus, nor is there any real inconsistency between Jesus' appeal to his miracles as signs and his refusal to give a sign that would be a compelling proof (Mk 8:11).

While Jesus' words and actions show that he regarded his miracles as truly signs "to those who had eyes to see," (Mk 8:18), he refused to work wonders to compel belief or to satisfy curiosity. Clearly the verb "see" also has a deeper, spiritual meaning. In this age the *dunamis* is veiled but it can be "seen" by those who have the eyes of faith. The early Church regarded the miracles as it regarded the parables, namely, as revelations or signs to those to whom it was given to know the mystery of the Kingdom of God (Mk 4:11). To the "outsider" the miracles were mere portents, the acts of one wonder-worker amongst many; to the believer they were unique—not so much in outward form or action, as in their inner spiritual significance as works of God.

---

[6]*The Gospel according to Saint Mark*, (Cambridge: Cambridge University Press, 1959), p. 83.

CHAPTER 10

KINGDOMS IN CONFLICT

THERE IS A MYSTERY in Mark's gospel but it does not seem to be a "messianic secret" as that idea was first advanced, to solve a problem of christology or apologetics. Rather Mark writes to remind his Christian readers of the mysterious nature of something they are beginning to take for granted. There is an ambiguity about Jesus' nature and mission and on both time frames, that of Jesus' own time and that of the Church; an ambiguity that can be overcome only by faith. By means of his strange ending Mark transfers the ambiguity from the first time frame to the second. Even after the resurrection the women are filled with fear and trembling and do not fulfill the command given them. The Christian may no more succeed in recognizing Jesus in the events of his time than the disciples did in theirs.

While it will not do to ignore the fact that non-Christian parallels exist or to deny their importance, in comparing the three classes of story—Christian, Jewish, and pagan—C. K. Barrett stresses the fact that "one is at once aware of the uniqueness of the narratives about Jesus, while the parallels have to be sought for."[1] The reason for this is that the gospel miracles draw their significance not from

[1] *Holy Spirit and Gospel Tradition*, (London: S.P.C.K., 1958), p. 57.

their content but from their context. It is the eschatological setting in which they are placed which differentiates these miracle accounts from other narratives which, both in content and in form, may be similar, and indeed almost identical.

Rabbinic and pagan miracle stories have taught us much regarding the form of these narratives. However there is a difference between the gospel miracles and the Hellenistic wonders or exorcisms. The former are not only wonders, they are signs, signs of the presence of the eschatological age. The things which many prophets and righteous men had desired to see and hear are now presented to the eyes and ears of Jesus' disciples. Both Jesus' powerful acts and his preaching of the Kingdom of God are alike witnesses to the fact that the Age of Promise has dawned.

Clash Between Two Kingdoms

On a par with his preaching, Jesus' miracles are the revelation of the Kingdom of God which is about to dawn. Whether through the one or through the other, it is God who calls forth faith. The dawning of the Kingdom of God signifies, at the same time, that the kingdom of Satan is on the wane. And so, the miracles of Jesus, as can be seen especially in the casting out of demons, are part of the struggle against Satan, the primary instigator of all the evils in the world. It is in pursuit of this last idea that we shall come to the most comprehensive picture of the role of miracles in Markan theology. They are one aspect of a clash between two kingdoms that runs throughout the gospel and in both time frames.

The clash between the two Kingdoms is carefully prepared for already in the prologue. Two motives are evidently at work there: a distinction of John's ministry from previous Judaism and a distinction of Jesus' ministry from John's. The beginning of the good news about Jesus Christ (1:1) is the ministry of John, while Jesus' ministry begins only "after John was arrested," (1:14). The "beginning of the good news" is announced in 1:1, but the "preaching of the gospel" is mentioned only at the second introduction (vv. 14-15).

The relationship and contrast between John and Jesus is also stated in terms of two kinds of baptism. It is those whom John baptized who are to receive Jesus' baptism, and his is to be a baptism in the Spirit. References to the Spirit unite the three parts of the prologue (John the Baptist, baptism of Jesus, and Jesus' testing in the wilderness). John says that the one coming after him is mightier than he and that he would baptize in the Spirit. At Jesus' baptism the Spirit descends upon Jesus. Finally the Spirit drives Jesus into the wilderness where he joins combat with the spirit of evil. Jesus is progressively introduced into a cosmic realm and combat with the power of evil. By "cosmic realm" is meant that "which transcends historical immanence and yet participates in the history Mark records."[2]

Testing in the Wilderness

It is significant that the temptation is combined with the account of Jesus' baptism. Rather than separating Jesus from historical involvement with its ambiguity and cost, the Spirit takes Jesus directly into encounter with evil in the person of its cosmic head. Thus the shift from historical to cosmic language has not entailed a shift from historical involvement to mysticism or otherworldliness. Rather the cosmic language only serves to accentuate the ultimate significance of the engagement. An essential part of the eschatological hope is the overthrow of the devil.

The tenor of eschatological thought dictates Jesus' temptation by Satan in the wilderness. The summary of Jesus' preaching in Galilee, as recorded by St. Mark at 1:15, opens with the words: "The time is fulfilled, the kingdom of God is at hand." Here we need to recall the general

---

[2]James M. Robinson, *The Problem of History in Mark*, (Naperville: Allenson, 1957), Studies in Biblical Theology No. 21, p. 33.

apocalyptic expectation that the triumph of the Messiah would be achieved only as the result of a peculiarly intense conflict with the forces of evil.

Furthermore the story of Jesus' testing in the wilderness is very closely connected with what has gone before in the prologue. There we learned that Jesus is the Messiah, the representative of the new Israel, and that he finds full favor in God's sight. "The old Israel was tempted forty years in the wilderness, and fell short of God's good pleasure. The implication of the narrative is that our Lord, like the Israel of old, also undergoes temptation, in this case for forty days, in the wilderness; but that, whereas the latter failed, he is now victorious. Accordingly, he is able to enter on his ministry with the declaration that the hour has struck; the kingdom of God is now at least on the horizon."[3]

From this starting point a clash of two kingdoms runs through all the rest of Mark's gospel and on both time planes. The struggle begun in the wilderness is continued in Jesus' struggle with the non-understanding of his disciples, and in the conflicts with his adversaries. It ends, seemingly, with Jesus' crucifixion, but Jesus then is vindicated by his resurrection. Finally Mark intimates to his Christian readers that the same conflict continues in the challenge to their faith. "The struggle which took place in the temptation continues in the exorcisms of the Marcan narrative, and the single event of the temptation becomes in the exorcisms an extended history of redemptive significance. This fact is of some relevance for the discussion in a subsequent chapter of history after A.D. 30 in Mark."[4]

The Debates

After action and character the third most important element in tragedy was *dianoia*, thought or intellectual content, and this intellectual element appeared especially

---

[3]Lightfoot, *History and Interpretation*, p. 66.
[4]Robinson, *Problem of History*, p. 30.

in the ideas expressed by the characters in discussion, debate, and conflict. The scenes of confrontation between Jesus and his opponents at the beginning of Mark's narrative come to mind. These are dramatically effective. The close succession of tense debates sets the action in motion as they cause discomfitted opponents to conspire against Jesus, and further confrontations are scattered throughout the narrative, keeping the action in motion.

These debates not only expound Christian doctrine, but they also enhance the stature of Jesus as he stands up to his detractors. By confuting them, he causes the action to move forward and the tension to increase as the protagonists entrench themselves more firmly in their respective positions. Such debates appear regularly in some of the early writers of tragedy and they became very pronounced in the Latin plays of Seneca, a contemporary of Jesus. Their abundance there would seem to indicate that they delighted first-century readers.

In Mark the Kingdom breathes the spirit of conflict and establishes itself over against adversaries on various fronts; a power struggle is taking place which erupts at successive junctures between Jesus and Satan, the Son of God and the demons, and the Son of Man and his earthly opponents. This conflict was initiated by Jesus himself in the wilderness confrontation. The Spirit-filled Son of God searched out and challenged Satan on his own ground. When he emerged from that contest he announced the advent of the Kingdom. Born out of a demonic power struggle, the Kingdom will henceforth assert its presence wherever the initial conflict is continued.

The Spirit

The Spirit is the element which binds together the three parts of Mark's introduction. In the Old Testament and Judaism the term Spirit had a strong accent upon the idea of power. John the Baptist says that the one who comes after him is mightier than he, and that he will baptize with the Spirit. When Jesus is baptized the Spirit descends upon him and later the Spirit drives him into the wilderness where he encounters Satan, the spirit of evil. In the synagogue at Capernaum Jesus encounters a man with an "unclean spirit," and expels that spirit. This is the first of the "miracles" that Mark relates, but the New Testament word for "miracle" is *dunamis*, "power, work of power." Later Jesus is accused of expelling demons because he is possessed by Beelzebul, the prince of demons. Not so, Jesus affirms. On the contrary, it is because he has bound the strong man (Satan) that he can enter the strong man's house and plunder his goods (3:27) by his acts of power (*dunameis*), the exorcisms and the healings.

In relation to Jesus' teaching with authority in the synagogue at Capernaum, the unclean spirit screams aloud. The spirit recognizes, quite properly from his perspective, that Jesus' mission is bent on overthrowing the demonic power structure: "Have you come to destroy *us*?" (1:24). Jesus came to crush not merely a single proponent of the powers of darkness, but the Kingdom of Evil proper. In response Jesus "rebukes" (*epitimao*) the spirit.

Far more is involved here, however, than a mere gesture of disapproval or a word of correction; this exorcism goes beyond the limits of a verbal confrontation. *Epitimao* connotes an aggressive effort to wrest the power away from an opponent. Jesus' command divests the spirit of his power and the spirit's defeat is signalled by the man's convulsions and a loud cry at the moment of exit. "What we witness is a physical power struggle between two diametrically opposed antagonists. Jesus' exorcising ministry amounts to a clash between two Kingdoms. As he brings his newly gained authority into play, and by actualizing his new word of teaching (which concerns the Kingdom!), he makes a reality of God's rule on earth. To do battle on behalf of the Kingdom of God is the intrinsic purpose of the exorcism."[5]

[5]Werner Kelber, *The Kingdom in Mark*, (Philadelphia: Fortress Press, 1974), pp. 15-16.

There exists a close affinity between Jesus' clash with Satan, the exorcisms, the healings, and the debates. So the Capernaum exorcism is immediately followed by the healing of Simon's mother-in-law, and the Markan summaries, by singling out exorcisms and healings (1:34; 3:10-11), likewise recognize the functional similarity between these two types of activity. The first miracle considered worthy of a theological reflection equal to that of the Capernaum exorcism is the healing of the leper (1:40-45). The condition of the sick man is not unlike that of the demoniacs. He begs Jesus to make him clean and Jesus responds by performing a cleansing. It is as though the leper was plagued by an unclean spirit. Because the disease brings Jesus once again face to face with the power of evil, Jesus is moved by a feeling of anger. Even after the healing Jesus harbors strong feelings toward the man and immediately orders him to depart. The general state of agitation and the forced exodus strike a clear parallel between an exorcism and a healing.

Exorcisms and Healings

Exorcisms and healings are the two principal approaches used to translate the Kingdom program into action. In both cases, Jesus intrudes upon enemy territory, challenges and subdues the forces of evil which are in the way of the fulfillment of the Kingdom of God. This is the manner in which Jesus mounts warfare in the first half of the gospel, so long as he moves about in Galilee. To the Christians, in the other superimposed time frame, this sounds a promising note. The disasters they experience carry no ultimate significance, for the real battle is still in process. The Kingdom of God is not lost, but at present crucially involved in combat against the Kingdom of Satan.

From the wilderness the clash between the two kingdoms moves to Jesus' exorcisms and healings, and from there into his debates with his opponents and disciples. The five controversy stories (2:1—3:6) have an evident "post-Easter" perspective. Mark probably chose to deal with forgiveness of sin, association with outcasts, the practice of fasting, and Sabbath observance because these were issues of vital concern to him and his people.

The healing of the paralytic (2:1-12) is a conflict report interjected into a miracle story (another Markan bracket). The emphasis is not on Jesus the miracle worker, but on Jesus who performs a miracle through the power of the forgiveness of sins, a claim to power which his opponents find scandalous. The Son of Man defends what in the eyes of the adversaries is outright blasphemy, i.e., the right to forgive sins on earth. In these stories conflict and miracle combined in creative interaction, whereby the miracle serves as a vehicle for the conflict. The healing miracle lays bare the dimensions of the conflict. The authority of the Son of Man exposes the opponents' hardness of heart and their murderous intentions. It is a life-and-death struggle and Jesus is to become the victim.

Non-understanding

In the first part of the gospel, Jesus refers repeatedly to the non-understanding of the disciples, but this confrontation comes to a head in the second part, after Peter's confesssion. This "confession" triggers an acute controversy which reveals that the messiah Peter was awaiting fell disastrously short of what Jesus had in mind. Jesus' prediction of his own passion and resurrection provokes an aggressive reaction on the part of Peter and Jesus in turn rebukes Peter for trying to lure him from the way of suffering and death. Jesus' suffering and rising Son of Man exposes the inadequacy of Peter's messiah, while Peter's refusal to embrace a suffering messiah earns him the title of Satan.

How close exorcisms and debates are is evident from the fact that Mark chose the exorcism in the synagogue at Capernaum to illustrate Jesus' unusual "teaching with authority," (1:22). This encounter with the demon includes

violent debate, so that its summary (1:27) not only repeats
the "authority" motif, but also repeats the concept of a "new
teaching." Thus Mark provides the exorcism as the pattern
for interpreting the debates in the synagogues. On the other
hand, the healing action is not the only important thing
in the exorcisms. This would be an all too medical interpretation of the exorcisms, and to this extent a moderniza-
tion. The exorcisms are also struggles of minds, or will, and
consist in words, as well as action. They culminate in an
authoritative saying, with which the issue is settled. All these
are points of similarity to the debates.

The exorcisms are drawn into close association with
the healings by the fact that diseases and other natural
evils were associated with the action of demons. Exorcisms
and debates are also close. Just as there are traces of exorcism language in the healing stories, there are equally
clear indications in the debates that they too are the actions
of Satan. The debates with the Jewish authorities are
designated "temptations" (8:11; 10:2; 12:15), thus making
their diabolic instigation clear. The debates with the
disciples concerning the necessity for Jesus to suffer are
put into this context by the pointed attribution of the
disciples' attitude to Satan (8:33), and the designation of
the danger to which they are exposed in view of the passion
as "temptation" (14:38).

Battle Over, War Continues

Mark's gospel ends with dramatic suddenness, with
Jesus' vindication at the resurrection. Jesus triumphs in the
struggle; is not the struggle then at an end? The two time
frames (contemporary and Christian) are superimposed in
such a way that the latter finds himself confronted by the
same challenge to faith that the former had to meet.

Certainly Jesus' struggle and his resurrection have saving
significance for Mark. But there were two ways this salvation could be imparted. The believer could either be saved
out of such a historical struggle as characterized Jesus'

career or he could be saved in that struggle. Strengthened by a power of hope lacking to those on the first time frame, the Christian could be expected to continue the struggle to the end. That Jesus chose the second alternative is indicated by Mark 10:30: "A hundredfold now in this time, houses and brothers and sisters and mothers and children and lands, *with persecutions*, and in the age to come eternal life." In spite of Jesus' resurrection and the eschatological existence of the believer, for Mark future aspects of the Kingdom still lie ahead.

Regarded from the viewpoint of eschatology, Mark began his gospel where he did because a new kind of history on a higher level began at this point. And Mark ended his gospel as he did because his eschatology implies a continuation within the Church of the same kind of history as characterized Jesus' history, i.e., a struggle between Spirit and Satan, until the final outcome of that struggle is reached and the goal of history attained. This is brought out especially in Mark 13, Jesus' Farewell Discourse. As James M. Robinson has written in his *Problem of History in Mark*, "the Church is seen as involved in experiences which are historical in nature, although these historical experiences are prophesied by Jesus, interpreted in the light of his experience, and seen as a commentary upon the exhortation to take up one's cross and follow him. The Christian is called upon to understand his history, not just his mystic or cultic experience, in the same way as he understands the history of Jesus. The statement (13:11) that the Holy Spirit will guide Christians in their defense before hostile courts is merely a confirmation of the fact which is already evident, that the struggle between the Spirit and Satan continues in the history of the Church."[6]

[6]*Problem of History*, p. 63.

CHAPTER 11
THE GREAT ASSURANCE

IN THE FIRST HALF of Mark, Jesus' miracles are the center of attention, and they amaze and astonish. In the second half Jesus' teaching, and specifically his teaching about the cross, is the center of attention, and this teaching elicits astonishment and even dissent. And yet, from the beginning Jesus is presented as a teacher. He begins his ministry "preaching the gospel of God," (1:14). He entered the synagogue at Capernaum "and taught. And they were astonished at his teaching," (1:21-22). *Didaskalos* occurs eleven times in Mark's gospel with reference to Jesus. Yet even in Mark 4, the parable chapter, it does not seem to be Mark's primary purpose to give us a sample of Jesus' teaching. As we have seen, the first half of Mark's gospel concentrates on the *kerygma*; the *didache* is reserved for the second half.

What then is Mark's primary purpose in Chapter 4? By his teaching and especially by his miracles Jesus attracts disciples to himself, but these same activities stir up opposition and incomprehension on the part of the disciples. Jesus' first miracles call forth wonder and amazement. When Jesus goes to a lonely place to pray, the disciples go to call him back (to further messianic activity?). And soon we find Jesus in discussion "with the scribes of the Pharisees" (2:16) concerning points of the law (fasting, sabbath laws). After

Jesus worked his next miracle (man with the withered hand, 3:1-6), opposition quickly hardened with determination. "The Pharisees went out, and immediately held counsel with the Herodians against him, how to destroy him," (3:6). And before the end of this same chapter, a line of demarcation is established between "insiders and outsiders."

This note of conflict points to what may be Mark's primary purpose in the parable section: here he gives what Joachim Jeremias calls "The Great Assurance." The parable collection is presented against a background of doubt: doubts in the minds of Jesus' followers—can this Jesus really be the promised messiah? Yes, Jesus has been working miracles, but as we have seen, these were muted messianic signs, not compelling, open to a variety of interpretations. Doubts were also occasioned "by the meagreness of Jesus' following, the apparently ineffectual preaching (Mark 6:15 f.), the bitter hostility (Mark 3:6), and the increasing desertions (John 6:66). Did not all this contradict the claims of Jesus' mission?"[1]

The Parable Chapter

The parables (Sower, Seed Growing Secretly, Mustard Seed) were meant to offset these doubts, to give "the great assurance." "God's hour is coming: nay more, it has already begun. In his beginning the end is already implicit. No doubts with regard to his mission, no scorn, no lack of faith, no impatience, can make Jesus waver in his certainty that out of nothing, ignoring all failure, God is carrying on his beginnings to completion. All that is necessary is to take God seriously, to take him into account in spite of all outward appearance."[2]

R. H. Lightfoot holds a similar view regarding the purpose of the parable chapter. The parables and the sayings which accompany them are not narrated at this point in

---

[1]*The Parables of Jesus*, (New York: Charles Scribner's Sons, 1972), p. 151.
[2]*Ibid.*, p. 153.

order to give typical examples of Jesus' methods of teaching. "Varied as the parables and sayings are, they all strike one note: ultimate success in spite of manifold hindrance. When seed is sown in a field, very much is certain to be lost; but, equally, much will fall on good ground and will produce a harvest, and a great one, some of it of the highest quality. Again, a lamp is intended and destined to give forth its light, not to be obscured and useless. If treasure has to be hidden for a time, it is only in order that it may some day be produced; it does not remain concealed forever."[3]

The farmer has labors and troubles in plenty and many dangers threaten the seed. But if he is wise, he will not be consumed with daily anxiety about the growth of his crop. The earth—or, if we prefer, God—will give the silent, mysterious, all-important increase, culminating in the harvest. "The same note runs throughout; final success in spite of temporary hindrance; if a work or purpose be of God it cannot be defeated; rather, the temporary hindrance has its part to play," (*ibid.*).

Lightfoot had expressed the same opinion already in his earlier work *History and Interpretation in the Gospels*. The reason for the insertion of the parables at this point is probably not hard to see. Chapters 2 and 3 have been full of controversy, and there has been little to relieve the darkness of the gathering storm. Yet the gospel has opened with the proclamation of the arrival (in some sense) of the Kingdom of God. In the parable chapter a supreme confidence is expressed in the certain triumph of good, and of that Kingdom, which is tacitly identified with the cause and work of Jesus and of his followers. "Just as in chapter 13, the only other extensive section of teaching in this gospel, the purpose of the *private* instruction to the four disciples is to implant the conviction that the suffering which lies ahead is to find its explanation and denouement in the coming of the Son of man, identified silently with the person of the speaker, so in chapter 4 those who listen to Jesus, himself

[3]*Gospel Message of Mark*, p. 40.

now outside the synagogue, are assured of the silent but irresistible forces at work upon their side, as certain and unfailing as the works of nature, yet at the same time not to be perceived by all."[4]

Seed and Growth Parables

The parables involved are both seed or growth parables and parables of contrast. In fact, the two ideas are almost inseparable. In each case there is the contrast between a small beginning and a large result. The interest is not concentrated upon the process of growth in itself, but upon two stages in it, which are contrasted with each other. This corresponds to Jesus' concern that men neither speculate nor calculate about the course of eschatological events, but interpret the signs of the time which lead to repentance and conversion. Out of the most insignificant beginnings, invisible to human eye, God creates his mighty Kingdom, which embraces all the peoples of the world. But seed is also a symbol of resurrection. It is no mere coincidence that in the Talmud, Paul, John, and in I Clement, seed is the image of the resurrection, the symbol of mystery of life out of death.

The occasion of the utterance of the parables may be taken to be some expression of doubt concerning the mission of Jesus. "How differently the beginnings of the Messianic Age announced by Jesus appeared than was commonly expected! Could this wretched band, comprising so many disreputable characters, be the wedding-guests of God's redeemed community? 'Yes', says Jesus, 'it is. With the same compelling certainty that causes a tall shrub to grow out of a minute grain of mustard-seed, or a small piece of leaven to produce a vast mass of dough, will God's miraculous power cause my small band to swell into the mighty host of the people of God in the Messianic Age, embracing the Gentiles.'"[5]

[4]*History and Interpretation*, pp. 112-13.

[5]Jeremias, *Parables*, p. 149.

A word then about the three main parables. The sower went out to sow, and seed fell along the path, on rocky ground, among thorns, and into good soil, and the last yielded an abundant harvest. Here the traditional figurative language is important. The rich harvest symbolizes the greatness and glory of the assembly of the saved in the Kingdom of God, or more generally, the coming blessings. This rich harvest is contrasted to the things happening at the time of sowing and growth, when much of the seed was lost. This corresponds to the contrast between current Jewish eschatological expectations and the ministry of Jesus. In many ways Jesus' work might seem to be a failure without result, or at least without enduring result.

Look at the Sower!

In an essay on "The Parables of Growth" Nils Dahl has written that "the problem to which the parable of the Sower is directed is a special aspect of the problem with which all the parables of growth deal: Could Jesus be the Coming One, when in many respects it was quite apparent that he did not succeed in his work? Could this be the way in which the kingdom of God was to be inaugurated? The answer is: Look at the sower."[6] The sower enjoyed a rich harvest even though much of the seed was uselessly scattered. So Jesus' ministry in Israel often did not lead to anything, yet it was the condition for and the initial realization of the coming of the Kingdom of God. The Kingdom of God has not yet come in glory, but its powers are at work, its seed has been sown.

The parable of the Seed Growing Secretly (4:26-29) might be called more correctly the parable of the Patient Husbandman. The essential contrast is not between the passivity of the husbandman and the growth of the seed in general, but between his passivity during the time of growth and his haste to harvest at the moment the grain is ripe. The putting

[6]*Jesus in the Memory of the Early Church*, p. 162.

of the sickle to the ripened grain is a traditional metaphor for judgment at the end of the world. By pointing to the behavior of an ordinary farmer, Jesus illustrates the proper attitude toward the eschatological harvest. Although the seed has been planted, life goes on as usual until the eschatological end. It will come when the time is ripe, when the process leading up to it has reached its climax. It will not come any earlier, but then it will come without delay. Above all, it would be useless and meaningless to try to hasten its coming.

Unlike the Zealots, Jesus did not attempt to establish the Kingdom by revolutionary activity. Many asked: How can he be the Coming One? Can the Kingdom really be breaking in? The parable says that between the coming of the Kingdom and Jesus' ministry there is a relation similar to that between the harvest and the time of sowing and growth which must precede it. Jesus does not need to try to establish the Kingdom of God by political activity. The events of the final era have already begun to take place, the forces of the Kingdom are at work; when the time is ripe God will certainly intervene without delay, bring judgment and establish his Kingdom in glory. To urge that Jesus, if he was the Coming One, should engage in political activity would be as foolish as to press the husbandman to be active in order to make the grain grow or to urge him to reap it before harvest-time.

The smallness of the mustard seed was proverbial. So in the parable of the Mustard Seed the contrast is between the small seed and the great, tree-like plant. The mustard plant is a "tree" of this kind, and yet the seed from which it grows is minute. In the same way, the initial appearance of the coming, glorious Kingdom of God might seem quite insignificant. But despite the disparity of size there is an essential identity. The parable is, thus, not directed toward the final consummation, but emphasizes the organic unity between Jesus' present ministry in Israel and the future Kingdom of God.

The Smallest of Seeds

The Mustard Seed should not be understood as a promise of a general kind; it answered a question of paramount importance to Jesus' contemporaries. Israel expected a glorious Kingdom of God, one marked by military and political success; a universal kingdom, in which the heathen would seek shelter with Israel, its God and its Messiah. Of all this nothing was to be seen in the ministry of Jesus. Could what was happening really be the beginning of God's establishment of his Kingdom? The Baptist and his disciples were probably not the only ones who asked: "Are you he who is to come, or shall we look for another?" (Mt 11:3). The parable gives the answer: Look at the mustard seed; in spite of its smallness, a great shrub, providing shelter for the birds, grows out of it. The apparent insignificance of what is happening does not exclude the secret presence of the coming Kingdom.

Mark has related the three parables of growth to the saying about "the mystery of the kingdom of God" given to the disciples (Mk 4:11-12). The real message of these parables could, in fact, be grasped only by those who in faith had understood the mystery of the secret presence of the Kingdom. And this is just as true of Mark's readers as it was of Jesus' first disciples.

The kind of imagery used in the three parables is significant. Not that of marching armies, heroic deeds, and valorous exploits, but the humble, homely imagery of sowing, tilling, and harvest. The seed is scattered, falls, and lies on the ground, and meets a variety of fates. Instead of striking out, defiant and aggressive, the Kingdom of God appears lowly and vulnerable. The seed is subject to adversity, rejection, delays, and loss. The parables contain no promise of instant and universal triumph. If partial loss is stressed in the first parable, the notion of long delays and slow expansion is conveyed in the others. But a positive trait of the Kingdom is also described—that of irresistible growth. No matter how slowly, and however great the losses may be, the seed produces. Finally, the three parables depict the inevitability of a final success that is out of all proportion to the seemingly insignificant and precarious beginnings of the Kingdom. The seed that falls on good soil yields abundant fruit but such gains are relegated to the future. For the present on both time frames (that of Jesus' disciples and the life situation of the Markan Church) the Kingdom embodied in Jesus before the resurrection and represented by the Church after Easter is often ignored, rejected, or opposed. It often seems powerless and its demise is often predicted. Its fulfillment through the course of history includes humiliation and suffering.

CHAPTER 12
INSIDERS AND OUTSIDERS

"THE GREAT ASSURANCE" IS AN important aspect of Mark 4, the Parable Chapter, but much else emerges from an examination of the chapter as a whole and the context in which it is placed. In Mark Jesus delivers two major speeches, one in Galilee (Parables), one in Jerusalem (Farewell Discourse). The latter is provided with an introduction (13:1-4). At first sight, this does not seem to be true of the former. And yet, in 3:20-35, the section following the call of the Twelve and immediately preceding the speech, the theme of opposition is carried to a new peak and then linked to the layout of the Parable Chapter.

Jesus had gone up on the mountain and called to him "those whom he desired," to be with him and to be sent out to preach. Afterwards "he went home; and the crowd came together again, so that they could not even eat. And when his family heard it, they went out to seize him, for people were saying, 'He is beside himself.' And the scribes who came down from Jerusalem said, 'He is possessed by Beelzebul, and by the prince of demons he casts out the demons.' And he called them to him, and said to them in parables, 'How can Satan cast out Satan?'"

Two types of opposition forces arrive on the scene, the relatives of Jesus and the Jerusalem scribes. The family declares Jesus mentally deranged, while the delegation sent from Jerusalem suspects him of being possessed by Satan himself. Jesus responds to the Jerusalem charges by speaking for the first time "in parables" (*en parabolais*, 3:23a). While Jesus stays inside a house with a crowd sitting "about him," his own mother, brothers, and sisters are said to be "standing outside," asking for him "outside." Unexpectedly Jesus rejects his own blood relatives and instead identified "those about him" as those truly related to himself: "Whoever does the will of God is my brother, and sister, and mother" (vs. 35).

Thus, immediately preceding the Parable Chapter, a distinction is drawn between "insiders and outsiders." Then this same carefully drafted division reappears in the parable chapter. At the outset the parable of the Sower is addressed to a "very large crowd" (4:1b), and this is referred to as a teaching "in parables" (4:2a). Afterward, when Jesus is alone with "those about him with the Twelve" he initiates them into the hidden meaning of the parable. In the formulation "those about him" we recognize Mark's previous designation of the true community of believers (3:32a, 34a). And again, these insiders are marked off against "those outside" to whom everything occurs "in parables." Only the insiders, the disciples and those about Jesus, are granted full access to his message. If anyone can, surely they are the ones who should understand. But as the continuation of the drama will show, sometimes even the "insiders" do not understand.

The Opposition

Thus the opposition assumes an unexpected form. The dividing line does not naturally fall between friend and enemy, but consigns some of those who would above all others be expected to be on the inside, members of Jesus' own family, to the outside. Relatives and scribes have been joined in a shared hostility, and Mark produced this effect by another of his brackets. The debate with the scribes is bracketed by the episode concerning Jesus' relatives (3:20-21, 31-35). As a result, the house mentioned at the outset (3:20a) furnishes the crucial locale for the total scene, setting apart insiders from outsiders, while scribes and relatives are linked in opposition. And this strange break precedes the mystery speech. It is not until the disciples have been dissociated from the relatives and scribes that they are given the secret of the Kingdom of God.

In Mark 4 the parable of the Sower (vss. 3-9) is followed by the "Purpose of the Parables" passage (vss. 11-12), which is followed in turn by the interpretation of the parable of the Sower (vs. 14-20). David Daube has called attention to an established rabbinical parable pattern, Public Retort— Private Explanation, dating back to the first century, which may be reflected here in Mark. As found in rabbinical writings the pattern may be divided into four parts: 1) a question put by an opponent; 2) the public retort, mysterious if not misleading, sufficient to silence the questioner but not stating the truth in plain language; 3) when the opponent has gone, a demand by the followers for proper elucidation; and 4) the private explanation, the real answer clearly expressed.

The author of the Purpose of the Parables passage seems to have been familiar with the form. He arranges the private talk in the same manner: first a request of the disciples for explanation, then the explanation. And, the whole which he produces, i.e., the parable together with the private talk appended to it, involves the same division as the original form between the outside world, destined to grope in the dark, and the elect, alone worthy of enlightenment. "Actually," Daube writes, "he makes Jesus dwell on this division in the harshest terms: the outside world, Jesus says, is spoken to *in riddles* 'in order that they may see and not perceive, and not understand'. There is no justification for mitigating this statement by declaring *hina* due to a mistranslation from the Aramaic, as is done, for example, by T.

W. Manson. From the beginning, the form in question is anything but universalistic. The author who used it when he supplied the parables of the Sower and the Tares with interpretations may have over-emphasized the exclusion of 'those without' from knowledge and salvation; but, essentially, the idea had always been implicit in the form."[1]

The Mashal

Mashal/parabole has a number of meanings, from "proverb," "symbol," to "riddle," and it is in this latter sense that it is to be understood in the reference to the "outsiders." To the "insiders" the secret is revealed; those outside are confronted by riddles. The term *parabole* also included not only words heard which are not understood, but also events witnessed; it was a comprehensive term, labelling forms of speech and actions in so far as both kinds of activity were regarded as media through which the mystery of the Kingdom of God was finding expression, though in such a manner as to be hidden from those outside. The logion is not concerned exclusively with the parables of Jesus but with his preaching in general.

Indeed, Jesus is not said to *speak* in parables to outsiders, rather that everything *is* or *occurs* in *riddles* to the outsiders (*ta panta ginetai*). Therefore it is probably better to say that Mark 4:11-12 is not concerned with Jesus' preaching in general but with his *ministry* as a whole. The whole ministry is *en parabolais*, i.e., an enigma to outside recognition. This points beyond a specific theory on parables.

The condition of the outsiders in Mark 4 is indeed an ominous one. All aspects of Jesus' ministry happen for them in riddles, so that they see and do not perceive and hear but do not understand. But Mark's narrative has prepared us for people in such a condition. In the latter part of the preceding chapter (our preparation for the Parable Chapter) we met with the scribes who had come down from

[1] *The New Testament and Rabbinic Judaism*, (New York: Arno Press, 1973), p. 149.

Jerusalem, who were saying of Jesus, "He is possessed by Beelzebul." This passage is framed by two references to Jesus' family, who were saying, "He is beside himself." Commenting on the scribes' allegation, Jesus declared: "Whoever blasphemes against the Holy Spirit never has forgiveness, but is guilty of an eternal sin." (3:29).

Hide, to Reveal

The interpretation of the parable of the Sower is followed by the other two basic parables (Seed Growing Secretly and Mustard Seed) and a number of detached sayings. Particularly interesting is 4:22: "For there is nothing hid, except to be made manifest; nor is anything secret, except to come to light." This presents a difficulty for those who extract a perverse "Marcan parable theory" from vs. 11-12, i.e., that Jesus used parables to hide truth. Here (their opponents claim) is the correct view, that parables are meant to help the people understand. In some translations, such as the King James Version, the secondary clauses of vs. 22 ("except to be made manifest," "except to come to light") are in the future tense. These were interpreted to mean either that things kept secret are now revealed in Jesus or that all things will be revealed in God's time. "All those interpretations are, in my view," J. R. Kirkland has written, "wrongly based. The textual evidence indicates that the future tense is not implied in verse 22 at all; rather are the secondary clauses to be read as final (purposive). The point of the saying is that what is hidden is meant to be manifested *by the act of hiding it.* . . . A paradox is intended, one which *explains the use of parables*: Nothing is hidden (i.e., couched in 'riddles', *'cryptic sayings'*) except in order that (*hina*) it may thereby be revealed; nothing is concealed except in order that it may thereby come to light. This is a perfect paradox; and if there be anything more characteristic of Jesus' teaching than parables *per se*, it is paradox. Jesus' parables were not constructed to prevent anyone whatsoever from comprehending ('not under a peck-measure, or under a bed') but in

order that the truth ('light') might be clearly discerned."[2]
A parable is enigmatic in form but elucidatory in function. Or as defined by C. H. Dodd: "At its simplest the parable is a metaphor or simile drawn from nature or common life, arresting the hearer by its vividness or strangeness, and leaving the mind in sufficient doubt about its precise application to tease it into active thought."[3]

Concentric Structure

The concentric structure of Mark 4 (as propounded by B. Standaert) is easily discernible. The introduction (vss. 1-2) and the conclusion (vss. 33-34) taken into account, the development begins and ends with seed parables. Before the center: Sower, Purpose of the Parables, and Explanation (Phase 1, vss. 3-20); after the center: Seed Growing Secretly and Mustard Seed (Phase 3, vss. 26-32). The central passage (Phase 2, vss. 21-25) contains the Lamp, Exhortation to Listen, and Measure.

The theme of Phase 1 is Reception of the Word. Those who hear the message of God display different dispositions and each one to whom the Word is addressed is responsible for his hearing. Phase 3 offers a vision of history, from beginning to end, that is full of hope. The exhortations of Phase 1 are lacking: the theme is the nature of God's revelation. The seed images underline the internal necessity of belief and the announcement of the glorious fulfillment we can look forward to at the end.

These two themes (everything depends on man, everything depends on God), opposed but nonetheless united by the image of sowing, are also found in the central passage but in the inverse order and based on different images. The comparisons of the Lamp and the Measure are both borrowed from domestic life, which unites them and separates

[2]"The Earliest Understanding of Jesus' Use of Parables: Mark IV 10-12 in Context," *Novum Testamentum*, XIX (1977), 12-13.

[3]*The Parables of the Kingdom*, (New York: Scribner's, 1961), p. 16.

them from the seed parables. The dominant theme of Phase 1, the need to hear, is taken up in the central passage and developed in the second place ("The measure you give will be the measure you get; to him who has will more be given," vss. 24-25), while the theme of the last two parables is anticipated by the Lamp. All must come to the light, which cannot remain hidden (vss. 21-23).

This chiastic development is not without its meaning; the two themes held in paradoxical tension embrace the reality of Christian existence. The first theme insists on the Christian's responsibility in the reception that he gives to the Word, while the second underlines how everything grows and bears fruit "he knows not how," (vs. 27), and even in contradiction to first appearances. "On the other hand everything is decided in the moment of reception, and on the other everything is in the hands of God, from beginning to end. What is revealed in Jesus Christ, however humble and contemptible it may be, must of divine necessity come to its full manifestation, but there is complete responsibility of man in his attitude to this revelation and there will be judgment proportioned to the measure of the reception given to the message. Everything is to be feared and everything hoped for."[4] The same paradox is encountered in the thematic disposition of the central section of the gospel (8:27—9:13).

Free and Responsible

Indeed, the same paradox is contained already in Phase 1. There is a manifest contrast between the Sower and its Explanation, on the one hand, and Jesus' words concerning the Kingdom, on the other (vss. 11-12). The Sower is understood principally in an exhortative manner; the two imperatives which frame it (vss. 3, 9) and the application as a whole (vss. 13-20) bear this out. The word of vss. 11-12 is pronounced in a simple declarative way: "To you has been

---

4Standaert, p 213.

given...; for those outside, *everything happens* in parables." The scripture quotation which follows underlines the divine causality.

The difference between the two roles (God's and man's) creates a tension on the thematic level: everything happens as predicted, foreseen by God; and yet everything remains proportioned to man's reception. The reception is at one and the same time the gift of God and the fruit of the receptivity of the subject. Mark reminds his Christian readers that Jesus' message has been received by some and refused by others. The refusal on the part of the Jewish authorities was foreseen by God, yet it was their full responsibility. "So likewise, if the mystery of the Kingdom is given to the Christian community, this depends upon that community and is at the same time a gratuitous gift of God. Both a theology of history and a spiritual wisdom are involved in the paradox. The contradictory and even tragic nature of the Christian condition and of its history is summed up in the theological vision of which hope is the fundamental element."[5]

The same tension is seen in the repetition of the phrase, "He who has ears to hear, let him hear," (vss. 9, 23). "To have ears" means at one and the same time to possess something which you have been given (by nature, or by God; cf. 4:11: "To you has been given") and to dispose oneself to hear in a responsible manner. If a man is given ears, hearing is his responsibility; or, if you want to hear well, realize to what an extent your hearing is a gift.

The narrative conclusion of the chapter (vss. 33-34) contains the same apparently contradictory elements. The fact that Jesus does not speak without parables (vs. 34a) goes back to the theme of vss. 11-12, where the mystery is given to some and remains hidden, "happens in parables," for others. "As they were able to hear it," underlines the responsibility of those who accept the word.

Mark's parable chapter is, therefore, a concentric struc-

[5]Standaert, p. 215.

ture. Phase 1 is composed of three elements of which the extremities correspond and frame the central element (vss. 11-12); these verses in turn anticipate Phase 2 which is the core of the entire chapter. Phase 3 takes up again the seed imagery of Phase 1 but develops it making use of a theme in the central phase. The concentric development facilitates the arrangement of the ideas and themes and dramatizes their paradoxical nature.

CHAPTER 13
THE NARRATION OF MARK'S NARRATIVE

FOLLOWING THE TERMINOLOGY OF QUINTIL-IAN, B. Standaert divides Mark into introduction (prologue), narration, argumentation, denouement, and conclusion (epilogue). Having dealt with prologue and epilogue earlier, let us now see how Mark looks in the first of the principal parts, the narration, from the point of view of concentric development (cf. Standaert, pp. 281-297).

A narration should be characterized by sobriety. The narrator should be clear, brief, lively and interesting, to be sure, but objective. The facts are to be presented in as plausible a way as possible. This is the opening speech of a debate, the presentation of the facts in a trial. In Mark's gospel the narration runs from the withdrawal of John the Baptist after the baptism scene to the description of John's death (1:14—6:13).

While they are a well-defined unity, these six chapters, by the sequence of events which they contain, also lead the reader toward the most important affirmation of the following part, the argumentation, the very center of the gospel. There the principal themes are the identity of Jesus and the following of Christ. The narration serves as a preparation for the argumentation to the extent that it announces this double theme.

So our question regarding the narration in Mark is: to what extent does it reveal in advance and in an indirect fashion the identity of Jesus and how does it already state the theme of "following the Lord?" Or, to what extent does it correspond to Quintilian's advice to the orator to prepare the argumentation by some "seeds of proof sown" in the narration (*"ne illud quidem fuerit inutile semina quaedam probationum spargere." Institutio Oratoria* IV, II:54).

All this is from the rhetorical point of view. From the point of view of drama we may now ask: to what extent do the first six chapters introduce the tragic action in such a way that the reader can anticipate the outcome? Dramatists as well as orators made use of the device of "sowing seeds," *semina spargere.* To present a successful tragic denouement, the dramatist by discrete signals must enable the reader/ viewer to anticipate the end, yet at the same time keeping the outcome veiled, so that the recognition and the final reversal happen in a way that is both natural and surprising.

Certain elements in the narration prepare for the argumentation and others anticipate the denouement of the dramatic action. The latter include all the forms of resistance and opposition that Jesus encounters. Thus, for example, at the head of the narration we have the call of the first four disciples (1:16-20). Thus the motif of following is introduced at the beginning and reappears in the two other sequences (calling of the Twelve and sending of the Twelve) around which the narration is organized. One of the essential aspects of the role of the disciples in the narration is that of an unconditional commitment to follow Jesus, to the point of coming to resemble him. The promise to make them "fishers of men" (vs. 17) is realized progressively as the narration advances. The motif of "following in the footsteps of Jesus" which is one of the two principal themes of the argumentation, is clearly announced from the beginning of the narration.

Other elements in the narration anticipate the denouement of the dramatic action. Thus the vocation and mission of the Twelve (3:13-19) contains an ominous note. After mentioning Judas Iscariot, the narrator adds that it was he "who betrayed him." This echoes the conclusion of the preceding section (3:6) and it also announces the denouement of the drama. The passage also contains a note of tragic irony. Jesus "called to him those whom he desired" and among them the one "who betrayed him."

A number of ominous foreshadowings are found also in the debates with opponents (2:1—3:6). Without apparent relationship with the context Jesus speaks of the moment when "the bridegroom is taken away," and in the conclusion of the passage on new wine and old wineskins it is possible to see an allusion to both his own end and to that of the opposition: "The wine will burst the skins, and the wine is lost, and so are the skins; but new wine is for fresh skins," (2:22). In the discussion about healing on the sabbath Jesus asks: "Is it lawful on the sabbath to save life or to kill," just before the Pharisees and the Herodians hold counsel "how to destroy him" (3:6).

Denouement Anticipated

Thus we see that the narration both prepares the center, the argumentation, and announces the denouement of the dramatic action. The two great themes of argumentation, the question of the identity of Jesus and the requirement to walk in his footsteps, arise in section after section with an impressive constancy. Also the process of "sowing seeds"— according to the expression of Quintilian—anticipating the argumentation, is clearly evident in Mark. From the dramatic point of view, the account keeps our attention focused on the tragic issue which threatens the protagonist.

The differences of point of view between the readers of the gospel and the persons involved in the account permit all kinds of narrative effects. Jesus' meetings with the demoniacs are particularly instructive on this point: for the reader, informed by the prologue, they reveal Jesus' identity without possibility of doubt and also the power conferred upon him by the Holy Spirit; for the characters in the account, everything remains enveloped in a certain ambiguity which makes it possible for them to adopt widely divergent positions. Scenes where demons pronounce the name of Jesus are lacking from this point on. Their function of indirectly revealing Jesus' identity is accomplished with the end of the narration.

We have also noted a striking parallel between the opposition of the Jewish authorities, presented in Chapters 2-3 and the attitude of the audience of Jesus' instruction in Chapter 4. This aspect of the role of the disciples will even be accentuated in the central part of the gospel (6:14—10:52). This parallel indicates the complexity of Mark's undertaking. To the extent that he wished to instruct Christians in the faith, he offered them an instruction, and that is the didactic part of his account; to the extent that he wished to report past events, he recounts Jesus' tragic history, and this is the dramatic aspect of his work. By dramatizing the role of the disciples, he succeeds in unifying his undertaking, yet his account still bears the imprint of two distinct genres: a *teaching* which follows from the discourse, and *history*, which by its intrigue and tragic denouement, follows from the dramatic action.

CHAPTER 14
THE DISCIPLES'
INCOMPREHENSION

AFTER THE FIRST PERIOD OF MINISTRY described in Chapter 1 (proclamation, calling of disciples, miracles) Mark relates that "in the morning, a great while before day, Jesus rose and went out to a lonely place, and there he prayed. And Simon and those who were with him followed him, and they found him and said to him, 'Every one is searching for you,'" (vss. 35-37).

In the light of how things developed later, one senses here that Peter was thinking that Jesus could be using his time more profitably; that he was more interested in messianic miracles than solitary prayer. If this were the case it would be the first instance of the disciples' failure to understand what kind of messiah Jesus was. Then the insider/outsider division is introduced in Chapter 3, to be taken up again in the next chapter, in the Purpose of the Parables passage. This in turn is followed by another reference to the disciples' incomprehension; indeed, more than a reference, an exclamation of surprise. "Do you not understand this parable? How then will you understand all the parables?" (4:13). And in the calming of the storm passage with which Chapter 4 ends, Jesus said: "Why are you afraid? Have you no faith?" (vs. 40).

The non-understanding of the disciples is the theme which ties together the material between Chapter 4 and the middle of the gospel. Non-understanding is found in four passages, and clustered around these references are three other significant elements: a bread or feeding miracle, a miracle on the sea (stilling the storm), and withdrawal into Gentile territory. When the four passages with their various elements are reduced to a table they somewhat resemble a structuralist syntagm-paradigm grid.

Mark 4: Parables	—	—	Non Understanding	—
Mark 6: Feeding 5,000	Bread	Sea Stilling storm	Non Understanding	—
Mark 7: Traditions of Elders	—	—	Non Understanding	Gentile Territory
Mark 8: Feeding 4,000	Bread	Sea Stilling storm	Non Understanding	Gentile Territory

Following the idea of a concentric development and tying ends together, B. Standaert splits this pattern, placing the first half at the end of the narration and the second half at the beginning of the argumentation. Quentin Quesnell, S.J., made a full-scale study of these passages in his *The Mind of Mark*.[1] A word then about each of the four non-understanding passages.

[1] *The Mind of Mark*, Interpretation and Method through the Exegesis of Mark 6, 52, (Rome: Pontifical Biblical Institute, 1969).

Four Related Passages

1) The Parables, Mark 4. After Jesus assures the disciples that the mystery of the Kingdom of God has been given to them, he returns to their question about the meaning of the parable of the sower. He declares: "Do you not understand this parable? How then will you understand all the parables?" (4:13). And Jesus' expression of surprise and sorrow is unexpected, since it is in no way unusual that a parable should need an explanation. Q. Quesnell observes regarding this passage: "The parables do contain some mystery worthy of the treatment they receive in the setting of Ch. 4. In all probability it is a mystery which Mark expected the formed Christian to recognize when he heard it referred to even indirectly." (p. 88).

2) The Feeding of the Five Thousand. This passage ends with the energetic declaration: "For they did not understand about the loaves, but their hearts were hardened," (6:52). The saying serves no identifiable function in the pericope in which it stands. The reference to "the breads" takes the reader outside the story of the walking on water. And "their hearts were hardened" remains inexplicable. Verse 51 would provide a perfectly normal and expected closure for the pericope. The self-revelation of Christ on the water and the sudden stilling of the storm would normally suffice to produce extreme amazement on the part of witnesses. No further explanation of this amazement is needed or even helpful.

3) The Tradition of the Elders passage. After the Feeding of the Five Thousand, Jesus goes to the land of Gennesaret and there the Pharisees, with some of the scribes who had come from Jerusalem, engage him in discussion about the traditions of the elders, especially hand-washing. Jesus declares that they make void the word of God through their traditions. And he "called the people to him again, and said to them, 'Hear me, all of you, and understand: there is nothing outside a man which by going into him can defile him,'" (7:14-15). The scribes took occasion from a single

instance of not-washing to pass judgment on Jesus' disciples as violators of *tradition* for eating with "*common*" hands. Mark takes the occasion to pass a Christian judgment on their *tradition* in vs. 6-13, ending with the affirmation "You make void the word of God through your tradition." Then he gives a Christian explanation of what "*common*" really means (vs. 14-23): "Nothing outside a man can defile him."

Here the Mark-reader level prevails (story as distinct from discourse). Mark is "writing from completely within a Christian point of view, which knows itself no more bound to 'the tradition of the elders' than to the law of circumcision (never mentioned in Mark, and commonly supposed settled among Christians long before any probable date for the final redaction of Mark) . . . Even in writing about historical personages (Christ and the disciples) Mark is not trying primarily to show how they answered this objection at a given time and place, but is concentrating primarily on giving dramatic presentation of Christian doctrine about Pharisaic tradition and about false and true defilement."[2]

It is important to note that after the discussion about hand-washing, there is a transition to Gentile territory. Jesus went "to the region of Tyre and Sidon" and had his encounter with the Greek woman, "a Syrophoenician by birth." Against the background of discussion about ritual purity, the woman is satisfied with crumbs from the table. Then Jesus proceeds into the region of the Decapolis and opens the ears of a deaf man. Then follows our fourth passage.

4) The Feeding of the Four Thousand. There follows a second feeding in a desert place, and a second incident on the sea, which again leads to a discussion about bread and non-understanding. And here (8:14-21) the tone becomes vehement, even startling: "Now they had forgotten to bring bread; and they had only one loaf with them in the boat. And he cautioned them, saying, 'Take heed, beware of the leaven of the Pharisees and the leaven of Herod.' And they

[2]*Ibid.*, p. 95.

discussed it with one another, saying, 'We have no bread.' And being aware of it, Jesus said to them, 'Why do you discuss the fact that you have no bread? Do you not yet perceive or understand? Are your hearts hardened? And do you not remember? When I broke the five loaves for the five thousand, how many baskets full of broken pieces did you take up?' They said to him, 'Twelve.' 'And the seven for the four thousand, how many baskets full of broken pieces did you take up?' And they said to him, 'Seven.' And he said to them, 'Do you not yet understand?' " The sudden transition to "breads" remains as inexplicable and as enigmatic here as it did after the earlier miracle, the feeding of the five thousand.

After the fourth passage with which we are concerned Jesus goes to Bethsaida (Peter's hometown) and cures a blind man. And this cure takes place in stages. Jesus lays his hand upon him and asks him: "Do you see anything?" The blind man answers: "I see men; but they look like trees, walking." Jesus lays his hands upon him a second time, "and he looked intently and was restored, and saw everything clearly," (8:25). And with this we arrive at the middle of the gospel, when Peter's eyes are opened, partially at least.

Before we pass on we should note that the cure of the blind man at Bethsaida is the first part of another of Mark's most effective brackets. After Peter's confession at Caesarea Philippi Jesus' journey to Jerusalem begins, and another healing of a blind man takes place at the end of that journey, at Jericho. And it is on this journey to Jerusalem that Jesus imparts his teaching on discipleship. What Jesus does at the beginning and the end he is in effect doing all along his way to the city—opening the eyes of his disciples to the full dimensions of his messiahship and their discipleship.

Treated in Same Way

Certain resemblances in vocabulary, persons, and general situation are to be observed in the series of passages delineated. Each of the parallel passages examined contains a rebuke of the non-understanding of the disciples which is hard to justify from the given occasion alone, and in at least two of the instances seems out of all proportion to the error they have committed. Even the first two, read a naturalistic way, would seem to make Jesus unfair in his judgment of the disciples. With what right does he express surprise at their ignorance? It is not at all obvious that the parable of Sower had the meaning indicated in the Interpretation, or that a statement like 7:15 ("nothing outside a man can defile him"), which went counter to the whole religious training and background of the disciples, should not need explanation.

All four passages include direct quotations from Old Testament material on the theme of the hearing and seeing and grasping of divine revelation as God's purely gratuitous gift; 6:52 uses the classic vocabulary of this sort of passage. Two of the passages explicitly point beyond the pericope in which they stand (6:52, 8:14). By reason of vocabulary, subject, and manner of treatment everything between 6:30 and 8:21 pulls together in the reader's mind. "At least this much can be said: the four passages are, as far as any one can judge, from one man and in that one man's head there is some reason why the 'mystery of the kingdom of God,' the knowledge of the parables, the Christian freedom from Jewish purity laws and understanding about the breads can all be treated in the same way. The same manner of treatment focuses attention on the mysteriousness and difficulty of each."[3]

Yet many questions remain unanswered. The explanations that Jesus gives leave the reader unsatisfied and the two comments on the breads offer no explanation at all. It is necessary to go a step further, searching for the intelligibility of the sequence in the light of the entire gospel. And to start with just two elements, why is it that parables and bread can be treated in the same way?

---

[3]*Ibid.*, p. 125.

Miracles and Parables

The breads, of course, stand for the breads of the two miraculous feedings, the 5,000 and the 4,000. This means then, for one thing, that miracles and parables can be treated in the same way. As we discovered in our treatment of miracles, they were not compelling proofs. "Their true significance is recognizable only by faith. They are, as it were, chinks in the curtain of the Son of God's hiddenness. The light let through the chinks is real light (the miracles do reveal, they are an effective manifestation of Christ's glory for those who believe (cf. Jn 2:11), and failure to discern their meaning and to respond to the summons to repentance which they constitute is without excuse...; but the light is not so direct as to be compelling."[4]

There are several reasons why it is not. Other people were credited with miracles; the amazement which the miracles cause is offset by the apparent weakness and unimpressiveness of him who works them; there were striking external similarities between many of Jesus' healing miracles and those attributed to others. "Thus other explanations lay close to hand besides that of faith: another prophet, another Rabbi, or even just another wonder-worker.... So the miracles are not inconsistent with the general veiledness or indirectness of God's self-disclosure in Jesus, nor is there any real inconsistency between Jesus' appeal to his miracles and his refusal to give a compelling proof in Mk 8:11f."[5] While Jesus refused to show a sign to the Pharisees, he nevertheless regarded his miracles as "signs." "Thus, the attitude of Jesus would seem to have been, on the one hand, the refusal to work wonders to compel belief or to satisfy curiosity, and on the other hand, the insistence that His miracles were truly signs *to those who had eyes to see.*"[6]

---

[4]C. Cranfield, *Saint Mark*, p. 83.

[5]*Ibid.*, p. 84.

[6]A. Richardson, *The Miracle Stories of the Gospels*, pp. 48-49.

Parables and Wisdom

Can we also bring that other element into conjunction with miracles and parables: "the Christian freedom from Jewish purity laws?" This refers to our third passage, 7:1-23, what we have been calling the "Tradition of the Elders" passage, following the *Oxford Annotated Bible*. Some commentators say that the main element in the passage is a *wisdom* saying and deal with the passage under that heading.

If we look at Mark 7 we see that Jesus has been debating the questions of the washing of hands and the Corban with the Pharisees and scribes alone, pointing out that what matters is not outward but inward cleanness, not the commandments of men but the commandment of God (vs. 1-13). Then we read: "And Jesus called the people to him again, and said to them, 'Hear me, all of you, and understand: there is nothing outside a man which by going into him can defile him; but the things which come out of man are what defile him.' And when he had entered the house, and left the people, his disciples asked him about the parable. And he said to them, 'Then are you also without understanding?'" (7:14-18). This is the familiar public retort—private explanation pattern. The passage begins with a Shema, "Hear, Listen," as does Mark 4, and the short saying which Jesus pronounces is called a "parable."

According to the norms of modern literary theory and criticism, the saying in question ("There is nothing outside a man which can defile him") is a periphrasis or circumlocution and not strictly a parable. But for the ancients, both Israelite and Greek, the term *masal* or *parabole* could be used of *any* speech that was out of the ordinary or in some way striking; the term was not restricted to the narrower class which is called "parable" in modern scholarship. In Israel it was used generally of obscure speech. The utterance about "nothing outside a man" could, then, be called a *parable* by Mark on more than one account. "First, as a wisdom saying, with its carefully wrought antithetic parallelism, it is not ordinary or everyday, but extraordinary and impressive speech. Second, it is speech that is not easy to understand, and this for two reasons. For one thing, periphrasis is reference to a thing in a roundabout and indirect way; the hearer must be attentive and perspicacious if he is to know what the thing is which is being referred to. For another, the metaphor implicit within this particular periphrasis gives to the saying two levels of meaning—and, again, the hearer might fail to arrive at the indirect but more important level. Thus a saying like this one could function much like a parable."[7]

Because they have not understood, the disciples, alone with Jesus, ask him about the saying "Nothing outside a man" (7:17), which he then expounds for them (vs. 18-23). This is in keeping with the public retort—private explanation pattern found also in the Parable Chapter. Yet Jesus rebukes them ("Then are you also without understanding?"), thus implying that, after all, they could and should have understood. The context of the saying, a discussion of outward and inward purity, should have provided the clue to its meaning; it could be comprehended by one who was willing to hear.

Miracles, parables, and wisdom sayings can all be treated in the same way. It remains to be seen how "understanding about the breads" works with these three.

[7]Madeleine Boucher, *The Mysterious Parable*, A Literary Study, (Washington, D.C.: Catholic Biblical Association of America, 1977), p. 61.

CHAPTER 15
ABOUT THE BREADS

THE MATERIAL IN MARK'S GOSPEL from the Parable Chapter (4) to the middle of the gospel is organized around the theme of non-understanding. The theme appears in four passages, which, as Q. Quesnell has written, are, "as far as any one can judge, from one man, and in that one man's head there is some reason why the 'mystery of the kingdom of God', and the knowledge of the parables, the Christian freedom from Jewish purity laws and understanding about the breads can all be treated in the same way."[1]

For one thing, this implies that miracles and parables can be treated in the same way. This was confirmed by our earlier treatment of miracles. The early Church regarded the miracles as it regarded the parables, namely, as revelations or signs to those to whom it was given to know the mystery of the kingdom of God. To the "outsider" the miracles were mere portents, the acts of one wonder-worker amongst many; to the believer they were unique—not so much in outward form or action as in their inner spiritual significance as eschatological signs.

The Mark 7 passage can also be included with this group

[1] *Mind of Mark*, p. 125.

because of the wisdom saying involved. While it is a periphrasis or circumlocution according to modern literary theory, it functions as a parable in Mark.

Hence it is that the three different elements in our four
passages can be treated in the same way. The parables,
wisdom sayings, and miracle stories all operate in a duel
way. Difficult to comprehend, they help to show why those
outside failed to recognize Jesus' messiahship; extraordinary speech, they are a striking and memorable way of
expressing Jesus' teaching to disciples and readers.
Moreover the indirect meaning which they convey often
eludes even the disciples, and their questions provide the
occasion for further teaching on Jesus' part.

About the Loaves

But how does 6:52 ("They did not understand about the
loaves, but their hearts were hardened") fit in? The connection between miracles and parables has emerged already.
Mark intends that the two feeding miracles, each of which is
followed by an incident on the lake (6:30-52 and 8:1-21), be
understood as in some way similar to the parables. This
intention is indicated by the conclusions to the two episodes.
The first ends: "they did not understand about the loaves,
but their hearts were hardened," (6:52); the second closes
with Jesus' rebuke to the disciples concerning the loaves:
"Do you not yet perceive or understand? Are your hearts
hardened? Having eyes do you not see, and having ears do
you not hear? And do you not remember?" and again, "Do
you not yet understand?" (8:17b-18, 21).

The feeding of the five thousand (6:30-44) is followed
immediately by Jesus' walking on the water (6:45-52). That
the feeding miracle has about it some meaning which the
disciples should have apprehended is clear, since it is
expressly stated in the verse just quoted (6:52) which brings
this pair of narratives to a close.

In Mark a plotted incident on the discourse level may
have a backward or forward reference. We find references to

events that occur before or after the incident (unit) in which the references occur. For example, after Jesus has expelled several demons, he is accused of doing this by demonic power. Jesus repudiates the idea and goes on to say that demons can be driven out only after Satan has been bound. Now Jesus has been driving demons out since shortly after the temptation (1:13). Therefore, within Mark's narrative world, Jesus' temptation (1:13) would seem to be the occasion on which Satan was bound. In the Parable Chapter, Mark 4, Jesus affirms that the secret of the Kingdom had been given to the intimate disciples (v. 10). In Mark's narrative world, this could only have happened in the calling of the disciples (1:16). From 4:10-12 on, the suspense about the kingdom is, therefore, suspense about the disciples' privileged knowledge of it, but also about their ignorance of Jesus' identity.

A Backward Reference

The non-understanding passages are such explicit backward references. As Norman Petersen has written: "In each case the reader is required to reflect back on previously plotted incidents in order to understand both them and what has transpired between them and the incidents in which the backward reference occurs. In each case the failure of the disciples to understand something in one incident is treated as the result of their failure to understand something in earlier incidents (see already 4:13). Consequently, corresponding to the diversion of suspense about the kingdom from Jesus to the disciples achieved in 4:10-12, we find that the plotting of incidents from 4:1—8:26 narrows this new focus by emphasizing the disciples' failure to understand the secret they have received—whatever that secret may be. Despite their privileged information they understand no more than others (cf. 4:10-13; 7:17). The poetic combination of the forward movement of episodes (heightened by anticipations of future episodes) with the backward references of some of them serve to involve the reader in a developing plot."[2] The non-understanding syntagm—paradigm functions for the reader, not for the actors.

But what is it that the reader (a formed but probably forgetful Christian) was supposed to glimpse in the passages? What is the meaning, or revelation, conveyed by the miracle which disciple and reader alike, were they not hard of heart, would perceive?

Twice we have feedings in a wilderness spot followed by a calming of the sea, both recognizable exodus elements. So, whatever else he may be doing, Mark is suggesting an eschatological realization of the original exodus. From their post-Easter perspective Mark's readers should connect this eschatological realization with the passion and resurrection of Jesus. The miracle of the loaves points to the Last Supper, and this in turn calls to mind its context, Jesus' passion and death. Significantly, in Mark's account, the breaking of the bread, symbol of Jesus' death, precedes the victory over water, symbol of the resurrection. As death and resurrection is followed by the missionary outreach of the Church, so the feeding in the wilderness place and calming of the waters is appropriately followed by journeys into Gentile territory.

Bread in the Wilderness

The account of the first feeding makes several allusions to the Old Testament. As a preface to the feeding, Mark says that Jesus had compassion on the crowd, for "they were like sheep without a shepherd" (vs. 34a), a frequent Old Testament simile. Mark then reports that Jesus "began to teach them many things" (vs. 34b), characteristically without specifying what he taught. The feeding of a crowd in a desert place evokes the exodus theme. It both looks backward to the feeding of the Israelites in a wilderness place and forward to the Last Supper.

Looking backward, the feeding of the crowd in a desert

[2]*Literary Criticism for New Testament Critics*, pp. 58-59.

place recalls the feeding of the Israelites in the wilderness. The two events are essentially the same: the miraculous provision of nourishment for a large number of people in a desert setting. The Markan term for "a lonely place" (*eremos topos*) echoes the LXX word for "wilderness" in the Exodus narrative (16:1). The incredulous question, how so many could be fed with so few resources (vs. 37), is a resonance of the similar question of the Numbers account (11:21). The orderly seating of the crowd may be based on the orderly arrangement of the Israelites during the wandering (Ex 18:13). If the Exodus event lies in the background, Mark's reference to "the green grass" (vs. 39) may be intended to indicate the Passover season. What is clear, looking back to the past is that in a lonely place the new leader or shepherd of the pilgrim people of God fed the newly pledged new Israel with miraculous food, as Moses had done before him.

Looking to the future, what is clear is that Mark could not write of the 5,000 or the 4,000 save in manifest Eucharistic terms: "Taking the loaves he looked up to heaven, and blessed, and broke and gave." But in the eloquent reserve of the evangelist, as John Marsh has written, "the difference between the 'new Moses' and the old is significant, though not stridently accented: Moses was not himself the feeder of Israel in the desert, and even though the manna prefigured the Eucharist, it was in essence food for the body; but Jesus was himself the feeder of the new Israel in the lonely place, and though the food was for physical satisfaction, its main significance was as the prefiguring of the Eucharist where the physical is made so overwhelmingly the vehicle of the spiritual."[3]

The miracle of the walking on water (6:45-52) is both an epiphany, manifesting in some way Jesus' being and status, and evokes another aspect of the exodus tradition, predicting a new and greater exodus. In Isaiah we read: " 'I am the

---

[3] *Peake's Commentary on the Bible*, (London: Thomas Nelson, 1962), pp. 760-61.

Lord, your Holy One, the Creator of Israel, your King.'
Thus says the Lord, who makes a way in the sea, a path in
the mighty waters," (43:16).

Whether the feeding and the walking on water were
joined in Mark's source or by Mark himself it would seem
that they are meant to be taken together on the literary level,
as they stand in the gospel. As Madeleine Boucher writes in
The Mysterious Parable: "If the disciples were terrified at
the sight of Jesus walking on the sea (vss. 49-50), it was
because of their inability to recognize him, which in turn
was owing to their failure to have grasped the meaning of
the feeding."[4] At the close of the two stories we read: "And
they were utterly astounded [i.e., at Jesus' walking on the
waves] for they did not understand about the loaves, but
their hearts were hardened," (vss. 51b-52). So we are left
with the question: what in the first miracle would have
yielded the clue to the second, or how are the two related?
And the question pertains to both time frames, that of the
disciples within the story, and that of the readers of Mark's
gospel.

Exodus of the End Time

All this falls within the scope of the exodus theme pro-
jected into the eschatological future. The eschatological
event would be a repetition of the exodus and wandering.
The idea of the endtime as a new exodus of salvation illuminates the Markan miracles of the loaves. "The disciples (and
readers) ought to have perceived in the feeding the repetition of the miracle of the manna. The event affords, in sum,
a glimpse into the mystery of the kingdom of God. It signifies that the new Exodus and redemptive event has begun.
The Markan miracle intends to teach that a greater than
Moses and the prophets is here, indeed, that Jesus is the
fulfillment of the law and the prophets, the agent of God's
final saving act in history."[5]

[4]Boucher, p. 73.

[5]*Ibid.*, p. 75.

The second feeding comes as a fitting climax to the first. Both disclose who Jesus is: the first is a veiled revelation, given to the disciples and the crowd; the second an epiphany, given to the disciples alone. Had the disciples penetrated the mystery of the first, the effectiveness of the second would have been greatly increased.

From their post-Easter perspective Mark's readers are intended to see yet further meaning. For them the pair of miracles should call to mind not only the exodus but also the passion and resurrection of Jesus. The miracles tie together the first and the final redemptive events: the exodus and the New Testament exodus, Jesus' resurrection. For Christians, Jesus' death and resurrection is the saving event which is the point of departure for the new exodus. Pointing to the Last Supper, a Passover meal, the miracle of the loaves also suggests its context, the passion. Christians know that at both meals bread is broken and distributed, that those who partake may have life in Jesus' body.

From the biblical symbolism of water, the sea miracle suggests the resurrection. The two miracles are joined in Mark to foreshadow the passion-resurrection. Readers are urged to understand the relation between the two miracles. The breaking of the bread, symbol of Jesus' death, precedes the victory over water, symbol of his resurrection. So the first part of Mark teaches in an obscure manner what is said plainly in the section which follows Peter's confession in Jesus' passion predictions. It is through suffering and death that the Messiah gives the gift of new life. The readers are asked to acknowledge Jesus' messiahship in the cross as in the empty tomb.

Foreshadowing of the Eucharist

For Mark's readers the miracle of the loaves would also be a foreshadowing of the Eucharist. The new manna given to the crowd in the feeding is made available to Christians in the Lord's Supper. Let Christian readers recognize the presence of Jesus in their eucharistic meals. Finally, miraculour feeding and the Eucharist together also anticipate the messianic banquet. At the celebration of the Lord's Supper Christians await Jesus' return, the appearance of the Risen One, with heightened expectation. An allusion in the sea miracle to the parousia and its homiletic lesson for Mark's community, which is experiencing adversity, is discernible.

The second miracle of the loaves and fish, the feeding of the four thousand (8:1-10), has much the same meaning as the first. As the first feeding was followed by a dispute with the Pharisees and scribes concerning ritual vs. ethical purity (7:1-23), so this one is followed immediately by an argument with the Pharisees concerning a sign from heaven, a compelling sign. Were the Pharisees given a sign of the kind they sought, faith would be precluded; if they possessed faith, they would understand that signs had been given them. The language of Mark suggests that the reader is to recall the hardness of heart of the Israelites during the desert wandering. "This generation" (vs. 12), by which is meant the Pharisees as typifying the Jewish people, is like the infamous "generation" of the exodus led by Moses. The pericope is therefore parallel to the Purpose of the Parables passage; both miracles and parables are challenges to faith.

Jesus says to the disciples, "Take heed, beware of the leaven of the Pharisees and the leaven of Herod" (vs. 15). The crux of the saying is the word "leaven." Whatever the specific sense of the metaphor, the saying calls to mind the Pharisees and the discussion about a sign from heaven in the preceding pericope, and suggests the general attitude of unbelief demonstrated there. It has to do with the resistance of "those outside" to acknowledging Jesus' messiahship.

The term "leaven" alludes to the leaven which was to be put away during Passover or the Feast of Unleavened Bread. Its effect therefore is to continue the themes of the feeding miracles: to a Christian reader, an allusion to Passover would suggest not only the exodus but Jesus' death and resurrection as well. The association of a warning against leaven and the idea of Christ as paschal lamb is explicit in 1 Cor: "Cleanse out the old leaven. . . . Christ our paschal lamb has been sacrificed," (5:6-8). Later Moses notes that the preparation for the Last Supper began "on the first day of Unleavened Bread," (14:12).

The Two Feedings

When Jesus recalls the two feedings he makes explicit reference to the number of loaves and baskets of broken pieces, using two different words for "basket": five loaves for five thousand and twelve baskets (*kophinos*) of pieces; and seven loaves for the four thousand and seven baskets (*spuris*) of pieces (8:19-21). The suggestion is probably correct that the two miracles signify salvation to Jews and Gentiles respectively. In the first story the number twelve represents the twelve apostles, and *kophinos* (6:43; 8:19) denotes a basket commonly used by Jews; in the second narrative the number seven represents the Hellenistic deacons (Acts 6:1-6) and *spuris* (8:8, 20) denotes an ordinary basket. This is confirmed by the structure of this section of the gospel (chs. 6-8).

Here we see Jesus move from the Jewish to the Gentile world; the first feeding takes place in Jewish, the second in Gentile, territory. "In this passage the readers and disciples are called upon to understand the universal destiny of the Gospel. Jesus' death is the sacrifice of the new covenant (14:24) by which a community is instituted composed of Jews and Gentiles whose fellowship is realized in their breaking bread together. As in the case of Jesus' abrogation of food laws (7:15, 18-23), the motif of the disciples' incomprehension is made effective by the fact that the Gentile mission developed in the post-Easter history of the Church."[6]

The feeding of the 5,000 is a Jewish feeding (twelve *kophinoi*) while the feeding of the 4,000 is a Gentile feeding (seven *spuridoi*). When Jesus and his disciples got into the boat Mark states that "they had only one loaf with them in the

[6]*Ibid.*, pp. 78-79.

boat" (8:14). In the following verses the phrases *artous ouk echousin* (or *echete*) appear. These have usually been translated "they (or you) have no bread." It has been suggested that these should be translated "they (or you) did not have several loaves of bread."

The One Loaf

" 'No bread' as a translation in 8:16 and 8:17 fails to take into consideration the plural form of the noun in contrast to the singular form 'one loaf' in 8:14. Further, the translation 'no bread' is nonsensical when it has just been stated that they had one loaf with them in the boat."[7] Jesus tells his disciples in this account that when he is present with them in the boat one loaf of bread is sufficient.

One loaf in the boat is all that is needed! In this instance, the "boat" is a symbol for the church, the Markan community. Separate bread (eucharistic or otherwise) is not needed for Jewish background followers of Jesus and for non-Jewish background followers of Jesus. The Markan community is an open society attempting to transcend social, ethnic, and economic boundaries. The passage may be taken as an early expression of open table fellowship for the followers of Jesus of both Jewish and Gentile origin. The one bread is more than adequate for all of their needs.

In the first half of Mark's gospel, therefore, there is found a theme of non-understanding centered on the disciples. The non-understanding touches on the teachings of Jesus, on his work, and on his identity. The theme recurrs repeatedly and this establishes an atmosphere of expectation. When will the disciples understand? The reader may also be reminded that the truths involved are not available to the natural man, but are gifts of God, for the reception of which one must be grateful. The stress upon non-understanding regarding the identity of Jesus also emphasizes the transcendent impor-

---

[7]Norman A. Beck, "Reclaiming a Biblical Text: The Mark 8:14-21 Discussion about Bread in the Boat," *Catholic Biblical Quarterly*, 43(1981), 53.

tance of the revelations and teachings which will complete the two themes (non-understanding and identity) in the second half of the gospel.

But they also seem to perform another function, perhaps even more important. They give the moral teaching of the second half of the gospel its full force and effectiveness as homiletic exhortation to the reader. Throughout the first half of the gospel the Christian reader can feel superior to the first disciples. They did not know who Jesus is but he does. They did not understand what deeper reality and message lay behind Jesus' teaching and actions, but the reader does know and does, at least in part, understand. By the time the disciples in the story receive the fourth rebuke for not understanding (8:17), the reader may feel rather securely on the "inside." Consequently he will go on to read the passion predictions which follow Caesarea Philippi in the same frame of mind, and be inclined to smile again at the imperfect and uncomprehending reactions of the disciples to these. But then, after each passion—resurrection announcement and subsequent instance of non-understanding and rebuke, there comes each time Jesus' words on what true discipleship implies. As a consequence, as Q. Quesnell writes, "the reader is suddenly forced to ask himself whether he has really understood after all. Has he made and begun to execute in his own life the absolute decisions which true understanding of the mystery of the cross and true appreciation of the identity of Jesus logically entail? He suddenly feels his superiority to the ignorant first disciples slipping away. The smiling self-confidence engendered in him by the earlier preparatory development makes him all the more exposed and vulnerable to the particularly deep-cutting piece of Christian paraenesis now directed at him. He must frankly ask himself whether he is not himself still caught in the same ignorance as were the first disciples."[8]

[8]Quesnell, pp. 171-72.

CHAPTER 16
JOURNEY TO JERUSALEM

AFTER THE SECOND FEEDING MIRACLE Jesus goes to Bethsaida, Peter's hometown. There he cures a blind man, but this miracle is special inasmuch as it is worked in stages. Jesus has to struggle as it were to overcome the disciples' blindness, lack of understanding, especially in the incidents which follow immediately.

At this point, 8:22, we have come to the midpoint of the gospel: the recognition scene. In response to Jesus' question, Peter declares: "You are the Christ." Then begins the one synoptic journey to Jerusalem, which ends with the arrival at Jericho, 10:46, where another cure of a blind man takes place. Thus a frame or bracket is established suggesting what Jesus is doing all along the way to Jerusalem.

No sooner does Peter acknowledge Jesus as Christ than Jesus brings that concept into conjunction with another, Son of Man (which happens also in the trial scene) and predicts his coming passion. Two other passion predictions are spaced out on the journey to Jerusalem. In each instance, teaching on discipleship follows, so that this teaching is given in a very special context.

From the Parable Chapter to the middle of the gospel (the Non-Understanding section, which includes the two feeding miracles) Mark is more interested in theological themes than in establishing a coherent itinerary for Jesus. Just as the first feeding was concluded by a departure to Bethsaida, so the second feeding and related incidents end when Jesus and the disciples land there. The healing of the blind man from Bethsaida is the only account in the New Testament which shows Jesus performing a miracle which is not successful on the first attempt. This account is more than the description of a miracle—it is a symbolic presentation of the healing of human blindness by Jesus.

Blind Man of Bethsaida

The conjunction of the cure with what immediately precedes (Jesus' complaint about the disciples' non-understanding after the second feeding) clearly indicates that Mark is continuing and amplifying his characterization of the blindness of the disciples begun as early as Chapter 4 (The Parable Chapter). Coming just before the great turning point of the gospel, the healing of the blind man and Peter's confession stand in some kind of symbolic relationship.

After the first healing techniques are applied, Jesus asks the man if he sees anything. He can see but his vision is imperfect and nearby men are out of focus. Jesus touches him again and he sees clearly. Mark's gospel was not written chiefly to provide biographical information about the life of Jesus but was designed to speak to the needs of Mark's church. Here Mark uses context very effectively. Sandwiched between two passages which provide pivotal descriptions of the blindness of the disciples (second feeding and Peter's confession), the context shows how Mark applies the blindness imagery to the situation of his own congregation. Mark draws a parallel between the myopia of Jesus' disciples and the spiritual blindness of his own contemporaries.

The Bethsaida cure is closely related to the whole Non-Understanding (Blindness) context which precedes.

Already in the Parable Chapter (4) readers are warned not to be too certain about their position as insiders. Insiders can be as blind as outsiders when it comes to understanding the Kingdom of God. The sea stories in the context (calming of wind and sea) portray the dangers of seeing and not seeing. Jesus' ability to still the wind and waves produces uncontrollable surges of fear rather than calm and causes the disciples to wonder who he really is (4:41). The calming after the first feeding presents the picture of believers who do not recognize Jesus in time of trouble because they are not looking for him. Even though they see him they think he is a *phantasma*. It is probably also a part of the non-understanding pattern that after the first multiplication of loaves, Jesus orders the disciples to go by boat to Bethsaida, but they land at Gennesaret (6:53). It is only after considerable wandering about that they arrive at their true destination, at Bethsaida.

In all this Mark's purpose is pastoral. The theme of blindness and sight has a positive side. The reader is to be warned and instructed by the shortcomings and failures of the disciples. Nonetheless those disciples are the foundation on which Jesus founded the Church. The fact that they get special teaching and are commissioned to cast out demons demonstrates that they are the true forerunners of the Church, which is also given the same gifts. After the harsh censures which follow the feedings, the cure at Bethsaida communicates a word of hope. Just as the second laying on of hands restores the man's sight, so Mark is confident that the blurred spiritual vision of his church will be corrected. And just as the cured man "looked intently" (intensive imperfect, vs. 25) so the Church will also see into all things clearly, and its new insight will be a continuing experience. The ability of Jesus to heal physical ailments points to a more important reality: the risen Christ will heal the spiritual blindness of those who follow him in the post-resurrection period. The Farewell Address (Ch. 13) predicts a great reversal. The disciples' error will become the error of the pseudo-Christs. The cure of the blind man of Bethsaida establishes the nature of the blindness of Mark's church and the way Mark believes it will be overcome.

A Half-Blind Confession

The key to the understanding of the Cure is found in its relationship to the Confession which follows. The blind man's imperfect vision corresponds to the disciples' understanding as it is depicted throughout the gospel. Jesus' rebukes addressed to the blind man are similar to other passages in the gospel where the disciples' ignorance and lack of faith is castigated. The disciples are not rebuked because they are using a messianic title which must be kept silent until a more appropriate time, but because despite all of the special teaching they have received they still do not know who Jesus is. Their incorrect confession enables Mark to show how Jesus is *not* to be proclaimed and gives him an opportunity to fill the Christ-title with its proper content. Jesus' rebukes here are similar to the one after the Transfiguration. There the disciples are ordered to silence because they are fearful (9:6), and because they do not understand Jesus' *logos* (vs. 10). In these verses Mark makes it clear that neither the disciples nor the church should preach about the glorified Jesus if they do not associate him with the Son of Man who suffers, dies and is raised from the dead (vss. 9, 12).

A Two-stage Healing

The two-stage healing of the blind man of Bethsaida portrays the experience of both the first disciples and the first Christians, and, indeed, of Christians of all ages. Throughout Mark's gospel the disciples have only imperfect spiritual vision, and although they have a measure of understanding they will require contact with Jesus a second time (the Resurrection) before they will see clearly. Mark depicts the partial blindness of the disciples in both halves of the gospel in order to make a comparison between the myopia of his church and the faulty sight of the disciples, but also to provide a word of encouragement to immature Christians. To quote E. S. Johnson: "'The gospel,' Mark is saying, 'is difficult to understand and you are not alone in your failure to comprehend Jesus. Even his own disciples did not fully grasp his miracles and teaching.' Although the disciples only have half-sight throughout Jesus' earthly life, the church knows that they did see clearly after the resurrection when they received the Holy Spirit (xiii. 11) and were reunited with the risen Lord."[1] It was these same dim-sighted disciples who successfully established the church of which Mark and his readers are a part. Mark is confident that just as the blind man and the disciples were eventually gifted with full vision, people in his church will also have their spiritual blindness removed. Their myopia will be turned to sight when they understand Jesus' teaching about his own suffering, death and resurrection and the meaning of true Christian discipleship. They will "see clearly" when they experience the presence of the risen Christ more fully in their own lives.

The Turning Point

Peter's confession at Caesarea Philippi is the decisive turning point in Mark's gospel. The differences between what precedes and what follows that turning point have appeared repeatedly. In the first part it often happened that teaching is not given where we might expect it. Now much more teaching will be given, especially teaching on discipleship.

Peter's confession (8:29) is the first occasion on which Jesus is called Messiah. Prior to this, Jesus has been gradually revealing himself by word and deed. The demons have recognized him as "the Holy One of God," "Son of God," and "Son of the Most High God"—regardless of what peo-

---

[1]"Mark viii. 22-26: The Blind Man from Bethsaida," *New Testament Studies*, 25(1979), 383.

ple present heard or understood. Peter's confession represents both a summary of what has preceded and the transition to a new phase of the story. Jesus' ministry in Galilee has ended; he now begins his fateful trip to Jerusalem. The story pauses for an evaluation, echoing an earlier question of the astounded disciples: "Who then can this be?"

"Who do you say that I am?" Peter answered him, "You are the Christ." Those who had witnessed Jesus' Galilean ministry consider him a prophet (or perhaps *the* prophet) because his ministry had been in the prophetic tradition. They have understood something—but they do not yet know the real secret of Jesus' identity. Peter's confession is presented as a contrast: "But who do you say I am?" Apparently until then no one had thought of Jesus as the Messiah; Peter's perception is something new. The contrast between Peter and the "others," as well as the importance the title "Christ" assumes later in the story, suggest that Peter is correct; Jesus is more than a prophet. Jesus' injunction to silence follows from the untimeliness of the confession rather than its truth.

Peter's confession of Jesus as Messiah is not the only signal that the revelation both of his identity (to the disciples) and of the meaning of that identity (to Mark's readers) has moved to another important stage. On this occasion, Jesus for the first time explicitly predicts his death. Mark's transitions are often abrupt, but his placement of the first passion prediction immediately after Peter's confession is a careful choice. Jesus' prediction of his impending death conflicts with Peter's image of Jesus as Messiah. Peter rebukes Jesus and in turn Jesus rebukes Peter, calling him a Satan (8:32-33). Peter's confession is another example of the mystery and ambiguity, the challenge to faith, that runs through Mark's gospel. Peter understands, yet he does not understand; he has seen something the crowds have not, but his understanding is still far from complete.

The Crucified Messiah

Jesus' rebuke has sometimes been taken to imply his total rejection of the messianic concept but the importance of the messianic titles at the beginning and end of the story do not support such an interpretation. Jesus is the Messiah and Peter came to recognize that, but Peter does not yet fully understand what that really means. The tension between Peter's confession and Jesus' prediction of his death appropriately reflects the contrast between traditional Jewish messianic conceptions and the Christian conception of Jesus as Messiah. At this point in the gospel, Mark seems to be leading the reader to arrive at a new definition of messiahship, a process that continues until the end of the story. Jesus is Christ, but he is the Christ who dies on a cross as a ransom for many; Jesus is the Messiah but a Crucified Messiah.

The first part of Mark's gospel is devoted to mighty works and teaching activity and this wins him a measure of success. But the real secret of Jesus' identity does not lie simply in his teaching or his miracles. In the second part, following Peter's confession, Mark portrays Jesus primarily as the one who must die. It is against a background of passion predictions that Jesus imparts most of his teaching on discipleship. The key to the reader's understanding of Jesus lies in his suffering and death. Yet, paradoxically, the prediction of these crucial events initiates the period of greatest misunderstanding, culminating in the flight of Jesus' disciples, so that at the time of his death Jesus is in a state of almost total abandonment.

On the Way

Moreover, the teaching on discipleship is imparted while Jesus and his disciples are "on their way," on the way to Jerusalem and this journey to Jerusalem is enclosed by one of Mark's effective brackets. Another cure of a blind man comes at the end of the journey to Jerusalem; the journey begins and ends with cures of blind men, the first at Beth-saida and the second at Jericho. "And they came to Beth-saida. And some people brought to him a blind man, and begged him to touch him," (8:22). Later "they came to Jericho; and as he was leaving Jericho with his disciples and a great multitude, Bartimaeus, a blind beggar, the son of Timaeus, was sitting by the roadside," (10:46). These care-fully placed framing stories are meant to qualify the whole intervening section, i.e., the healings cast light on the jour-ney to Jerusalem. What Jesus does at the beginning and end of the trip, open the eyes of blind men, he is in effect trying to do all along his way to the city. He strives to open the eyes of the disciples and initiate them into a new dimension of his messiahship.

Most of the miracle stories in Mark cluster in blocks in Chapters 5-8. Mark includes only two reports of Jesus' healing of blind men and these are strongly isolated; both are outside those clusters. The two healings of blind men have the same function as Jesus' other acts of power, but in addition they both have a pronounced figurative, illustra-tive function. Both occur at points in the story when the "blindness" of those around Jesus is most pronounced.

The first of the two stories occurs after the second feeding, just before Peter's confession. Jesus has just reproached his disciples for failing to understand the two feeding miracles ("Having eyes do you not see, and having ears do you not hear?"). Jesus lays his hands upon the blind man and he sees men but they look like trees walking. Jesus lays his hands upon the blind man again and he sees everything clearly. So Peter's confession that Jesus is the Christ indicates that he has "seen" something, although his inability to accept Jesus' suffering implies that he has not seen everything. Peter also needs two stages before his eyes will be completely opened.

The Blind Man Frame

Just before the healing of blind Bartimaeus at Jericho, Jesus' disciples were arguing about status, proving their continued lack of insight. After healing Bartimaeus, Jesus enters Jerusalem, to be rejected by the Jewish leaders, executed by the Romans, and mocked as "Christ, the King of Israel" and "King of the Jews." Yet blind Bartimaeus recognizes Jesus as the true "Son of David" (10:48). Those with eyes are blind, while the blind see.

In addition to the *inclusio* established by the two healings of blind men, Mark's central section is also placed into the framework of the "Way." At the outset Jesus and his disciples are reported to be "on the way" (8:27), and at the end Bartimaeus is said to have followed Jesus "on the way" (10:52), and interspersed throughout this midsection the Way motif is featured four more times. The disciples are twice said to have engaged in a discussion "on the way" (9:33, 34), Jesus continues traveling "along the way" (10:17), and toward the end of the section it is disclosed that he is "on the way" (10:32) to Jerusalem. The Way motif is definitely a Markan element: both Matthew and Luke consistently eliminate the references.

The Journey to Jerusalem is skillfully subdivided by three passion-resurrection predictions (8:31; 9:31; 10:33-34), each of which is placed into a different geographical locale. The first prediction is situated in the area of Caesarea Philippi (8:27), the second one is given in Galilee (9:30), and the third one on the way to Jerusalem (10:32). Three additional place names strategically spaced through the account further strengthen the effect of the Journey: Capernaum (9:33), the region of Judaea and beyond the Jordan (10:1), and Jericho (10:46).

Geographical Signposts

From a literary perspective, the formal ordering of the Journey section, the carefully set pattern of the predictions, and the pervasiveness of the Way motif reflect the understanding that there is order and purpose to Jesus' ministry. The underlying theme of the Way provides structure and meaning; Mark placed the two cures of blind men at the

margins of this section, and between them inserted topo-
graphical reference marks which mediate the movement
from one place to the other. By setting up geographical
signposts along this way, a journey is created that gives
direction to Jesus' life. The goal, Jerusalem, is announced
for the first time at the occasion of the third and last
passion–resurrection prediction (10:32, 33). The transition
from the Journey to the Jerusalem section proper (11:1)
announces Jesus' arrival in the vicinity of Jerusalem. The
journey is undertaken with the definite purpose of going to
Jerusalem.

The three Synoptics present Jesus' ministry according to
the same basic plan. Baptized in the Jordan, Jesus returns to
Galilee for his ministry of word and works, and makes one
journey to Jerusalem, the scene of his death. Mark 1-10
relates Jesus' preaching and healing ministry in Galilee,
Mark 11-15 relates his final confrontation with the Jewish
and Roman leaders in Jerusalem. The story ends with a
promise to return to Galilee after his resurrection (16:7).
Beyond this it is difficult to trace out Jesus' movements on a
map because so much is left out and geography is subordi-
nated to theology. The disciples' setting out for Bethsaida
and arriving at the land of Gennesaret may be part of their
non-understanding, and movement from Jewish to Gentile
territory is also suggestive. Above all, the movement from
Galilee to Jerusalem seems to be a significant pattern in
Mark's gospel. In John's gospel, Jesus visits Jerusalem fre-
quently, traveling to Galilee only when he encounters hostility in Judea (John 7:1-9). In Luke, Jesus appears in
Jerusalem to his disciples after the resurrection. Why,
according to Mark, does Jesus tell his disciples to meet him
in Galilee (14:28; 16:7)? For Mark, Galilee and Jerusalem
seem to serve as symbols as well as geographical locations.

"The variety of explanations scholars offer for Mark's
interest in Galilee indicates uncertainty as to its significance,
but that of Jerusalem is easier to appreciate. Jerusalem
symbolizes the climactic events toward which the Gospel's
story relentlessly moves. It is the religious capital of Israel,

the place where the Temple is located. It is also the seat of the religious and political authorities, who will, in the name of tradition and political stability, have Jesus arrested and executed. Jerusalem is important not simply as a location but as the place where Jesus will die."[2]

Early in the gospel, one hears rumblings from the storm gathering in Jerusalem. Even while Jesus is still in the north, the "scribes who came down from Jerusalem" (3:22) characterize him as a demoniac, and, in Chapter 6, the Pharisees and "some of the scribes, who had come from Jerusalem" verbally attack Jesus again. In 8:31, Jesus announces to his disciples that he is going to Jerusalem to die, a prediction repeated twice in subsequent chapters (9:31; 10:33). The inexorable movement toward Jerusalem, the place of death, helps to tie the story together.

[2]D. Juel, *Introduction to New Testament Literature*, p. 180.

CHAPTER 17

DISCIPLESHIP, FOLLOWING ON THE WAY

IN MARK'S GOSPEL most of the explicit teaching of Jesus is given in the second part, after Peter's confession at Caesarea Philippi, and that teaching is devoted especially to discipleship. It is imparted in close conjunction with the passion predictions, and it is imparted while Jesus and his disciples are "on the way" to Jerusalem, a journey which is bracketed by the healing of two blind men.

At Caesarea Philippi Peter acknowledges Jesus as the Christ. Immediately Jesus goes on to say that to be the Christ means to suffer—"He began to teach them that the Son of Man must suffer many things, be killed, and after three days rise again" (8:31). Then Jesus goes on to say that to be a Christian means to suffer—"If any man would come after me, let him deny himself and take up his cross and follow me" (v. 34). From the prediction of the Passion we move directly to the nature of discipleship. There are three such predictions and we find that the same is true of each of the other predictions. After the second (9:31) Jesus teaches that discipleship means service—"If any one would be first, he must be last of all and servant of all," (9:35). The nature of discipleship is thus set in the light of the Cross; the understanding of discipleship proceeds from an understanding of the Cross.

This gives us an additional reason why Mark chose to reserve the teaching on discipleship to a place toward the end of the gospel. The only way the disciples could discover who Jesus is and who they are was to walk the way of Jesus to the end. They could not understand Jesus prior to his cross and resurrection; therefore it is fitting that the teaching on discipleship should be imparted as Jesus and his disciples were walking toward the scene of those events.

The Way to the End

The non-understanding and incomprehension which characterize the disciples is never explicitly dispelled anywhere in the gospel. Even after the Transfiguration, Peter was confused and afraid. After the third passion prediction we are shown what was in the minds of the disciples at that time—ambition and status. It is only by subtle signals that we are made aware that the disciples' incomprehension was ever dispelled. In the Farewell Address Jesus speaks of a time when the disciples' error will become the error of their opponents, and the women at the tomb are instructed to tell the disciples that Jesus will meet them in Galilee to continue his mission through them. Otherwise the disciples' incomprehension is unbroken to the end. Despite all Jesus taught them, despite their intimate association with him, despite all they had seen him do, the disciples could not understand Jesus prior to his climactic fate on the cross.

In an article on "Mark as Interpreter of the Jesus Tradition," Paul Achtemeier draws the conclusion that there is "no Jesus without the cross, no Jesus without faith, no faith without a cross."[1] First, for Mark there is no real comprehension of Jesus apart from knowledge of his final fate on the cross and the subsequent resurrection. Thus the climax

[1] *Interpretation*, 32(1978), 352.

of Jesus' career becomes also the key to understanding that career, and the possibility of seeing primarily in Jesus anything other than the Crucified and Risen Lord is cut off. Secondly, if there is no Jesus without the cross, there is for us no Jesus apart from faith. Seeing is not enough. Jesus' words and deeds were marked by ambiguity, open to different interpretations, and that ambiguity is transferred to the time frame of Mark and his readers. If it could happen to those who saw and heard Jesus in person, is it any wonder that it remains possible to misunderstand Jesus? Christians must continue to walk by faith even on the Easter side of resurrection. The ambiguity that cloaked the earthly Jesus remains drawn over the Risen Jesus until his return in glory. Thirdly, there is no faith without the cross. "Whoever would save his life will lose it," (8:35). Discipleship cannot be built around self-fulfillment schemes; the goal of life is Christ, not self.

Jesus is an authoritative teacher who brings men to an understanding of the truth, but he is not just a Gnostic revealer who gives insight to the initiated. "The main purpose of his teaching is to bring his followers to an understanding of his own Cross, not only as redemptive, but also as a way of life for themselves; they must take up their crosses as he did and serve as he served. Thus it is not that he only enlightens their minds but that he calls for them to go on the way of discipleship, which is the way of love and service."[2]

Discipleship Foreshadowed

Most of Jesus' teaching is given after the midpoint of the gospel, but in the area of discipleship much is also given by way of foreshadowing. Soon after the action gets under way, Mark shows Jesus calling his first disciples. Passing along the Sea of Galilee Jesus saw Simon and Andrew

[2]Ernest Best, *The Temptation and the Passion: The Markan Soteriology*, (Cambridge: Cambridge University Press, 1965), p. 190.

casting a net and he said, "Follow me!" and immediately they left their nets and followed him. Similarly, James and John left their father and the hired servants and followed him (1:20).

Mark seems to have added this story in an effort to show in a concrete way what the call to discipleship could mean. Nothing is said about time or exact place, or about any other details. "The story is like a woodcut in that only the important features are presented. In the arrangement of his material Mark has created an impression that is far more important than such information as where or when the calls were issued or whether or not they occurred on the same day (cf. 6:7). The fewer the details told and the more closely it resembles an imaginary scene, the easier it is for the reader to find himself in the story."[3]

In Mark's narrative discipleship always begins with Jesus looking at a person and calling him. The call of the disciples is related without any indication that the fishermen might have had time for reflection or might have had to overcome certain difficulties before responding. In a very substantial way discipleship is a new manner of acting and thinking which is sustained by the event of grace. Those who are called have had no specific preparation, nor have they even necessarily been among those who heard Jesus' preaching. Jesus does not encounter men in some special religious sphere, but in the midst of everyday life where they really live. Men are made disciples by the call of Jesus, which is as powerful as the creative word of God and whatever those who are called may become will be the work of Jesus.

New Manner of Acting

Jesus' concept of discipleship is a new creation. The Greeks spoke of "disciples of God" but they meant by this "becoming like him" in an ethical sense, or the obedience to

[3]E. Schweizer, *The Good News according to Mark,* (Richmond: John Knox Press, 1970), p. 47.

his commandments. The relationship of the rabbis to their students is a closer parallel to Jesus' discipleship. But the rabbi did not call his disciples—he is sought by them. Above all, the rabbis never could have conceived of a call so radical as to make clear that being with Jesus is more important than all of God's commandments. The rich young man had observed all the commandments, yet Jesus said that he was still lacking something. "Sell what you have and come, follow me!" (10:21). This idea is found already in the first calling of the disciples.

A disciple of a rabbi might dream of some day becoming even better, if possible, than his master; but a disciple of Jesus could never expect that some day he himself might be the "Son of Man." Jesus never debates with his disciples as a rabbi would have done. Thus the word "follow" received a new sound when Jesus said it, a sound which it has nowhere else "except in those passages of the Old Testament which declare that one must follow either Baal or Yahweh (1 Kings 18:21; cf. the idea in Prov. 7:22)."[4]

Jesus calls the first disciples and they respond and the reader can respond positively to them during this phase of fidelity and understanding. But then signs of non-understanding begin to appear. When Jesus goes out to the wilderness place to pray at night, Peter and the others went out to "track him down," (1:36), probably the first sign of discrepancy between Jesus' and the disciples' concept of discipleship. Jesus marvels that the disciples could not understand the parable of the Sower, and complaints about the disciples incomprehension grow increasingly vehement up to the midpoint of the gospel, and incomprehension continues to be manifested during the journey to Jerusalem. And when the crisis comes, all the disciples eventually flee.

Risks of Discipleship

All this brings out another aspect of discipleship. To become a disciple is to expose oneself to risks—to the risk of

4*Ibid.*, p. 49.

hardship, misunderstanding, persecution, and, above all, to the risk of failure. People who remain on their own front porch don't run risks; it's the people who set out to scale high peaks who get involved in spectacular downfalls.

Jesus further expands his teaching on discipleship in the Gerasene demoniac incident. The man who had been possessed with demons begged him "that he might be with him," (5:18). But Jesus said to him: "Go home to your friends, and tell them how much the Lord has done for you,"(v. 19). This shows us that the "messianic secret" applied only under certain circumstances. But it also shows us "how impossible it is to have a stereotyped definition of discipleship. One person is taken away from home and family (1:16-20), another is sent back to them contrary to his own wishes. Discipleship is not a way of salvation by which the individual can secure his own happiness. The concern of discipleship is always how the Good News can best be proclaimed and passed on to others."[5]

Peter's confession at Caesarea Philippi comes at the midpoint of the gospel. " 'But who do you say that I am?' Peter answered him, 'You are the Christ,' " (8:29). Even at this point, Peter had not progressed as far as the demons, who, more correctly, called Jesus the Son of God (5:6 ff.). Then for the first time Jesus speaks openly and without parables about his passion and resurrection. The word had to become flesh in the body of the Crucified; otherwise he could not reach the hearts of men. But not even the disciples are able to understand the announcement of the passion.

Beyond the narrow circle of the disciples Jesus must summon all men to follow him on the way to the cross; this is the only place where God's action can be understood. Consequently, discipleship, which appeared already at the beginning of the public ministry, is the main topic of instruction while Jesus and his disciples are "on the way" to Jerusalem. In the course of this journey the word "follow" is used with special significance. Three times the announcement of

[5]*Ibid.*, p. 114.

the passion of the Son of Man is followed by the misunderstanding of the disciples and Jesus' call to discipleship. The section ends with the second half of the blind men bracket, and as a result a man "followed" Jesus on the road, the road to Jerusalem.

Each passion-resurrection prediction is followed by a discourse on discipleship and for the most part these conversations between Jesus and the disciples center around the qualifications of discipleship. While walking the way with Jesus, the disciples learn that true discipleship means to deny oneself, go take up one's cross, to lose one's life, to be last and least, to drink the cup that Jesus is to drink, and to be baptized with Jesus' baptism. This radical discipleship message is both preached and dramatically executed through the medium of the Way. By weaving the passion-resurrection predictions and the discipleship discourses together into the narration of the journey to Jerusalem, Mark weaves together the life of Jesus and the life of the disciple. The way of Jesus is the way of the disciple, and discipleship consists in walking the way of Jesus.

This is the meaning of the verb "to follow" in the gospel of Mark. Jesus leads the way and the disciples are to follow him; Jesus does not merely preach the way, but he literally shows the way. If they follow after Jesus leading on, "they will not only learn their leader's identity, but in the process find themselves and their own calling. Full knowledge of Jesus will give them insight into their own nature and destiny. But again, if they are to grasp Jesus and know themselves, they will have to go the way of Jesus, and they will have to walk it to the end. As the leader so are his followers called to walk through the strait gate of suffering to glory."[6]

Closing the Bracket

The healing of the blind Bartimaeus (10:46-52) is the second half of the blind men *inclusio* which brackets the trip

---

[6]W. Kelber, *Kingdom in Mark*, p. 71.

to Jerusalem. Taken together they indicate what Jesus was trying to do on the way to Jerusalem. But each also has its special emphasis. In the healing at Bethsaida (8:22-26) the primary emphasis is on the two-stage healing process and little attention is paid to the reaction of the man himself. The Jericho healing presents a lively portrait of a blind beggar who addresses Jesus with two different titles, persistently cries out for mercy, catches Jesus' ear despite attempts to silence him and finally follows him on the way.

Just as the Bethsaida healing terminates a series of passages in which the blindness of the disciples is graphically depicted, so the Jericho healing concludes a portion of the gospel which shows that despite Jesus' patient instruction his disciples are still unprepared for his journey to the cross. It also pulls together some key concepts introduced at the beginning of the gospel. John the Baptist must prepare the way, Bartimaeus follows Jesus in the way; the disciples leave their nets and follow Jesus, Bartimaeus leaves his beggar's cloak to follow Jesus; Jesus made faith a requirement for entry into the Kingdom, Bartimaeus is commended because his faith has saved him.

Bartimaeus is told: "Your faith has made you well." In his description of miracles Mark consistently moves from the miraculous to the kerygmatic. Thus the first miracle in the synagogue at Capernaum brackets the question, "What is this? A new teaching!" (1:27), and the most important result of the faith of the paralytic's friends is forgiveness of sin (2:5). "The miracles in which faith is a key factor are paradigmatic and are designed to assist the Christian as he or she struggles with doubt and unbelief. Mark is able to do this because the Christian reader knows that Jesus does more than heal part of a man—he can restore the whole person."[7]

Bartimaeus is "made well" by his faith and "immediately he received his sight," (vs. 52). Just as the reference to a faith that makes well implies more than belief in Jesus as a

[7]E. S. Johnson, Jr., "Mark 10:46-52: Blind Bartimaeus," *Catholic Biblical Quarterly*, 40(1979), 199.

wonderworker, so the context in which Mark sets the Jericho healing indicates that "to make well" there goes beyond its literal meaning of "heal" to that of "save," as is the case in a number of other passages.

These passages, which equate salvation with the granting of spiritual vision, provide a parallel to Mark's interpretation of the Bartimaeus passage and a key to the theme of blindness and sight which he develops throughout the gospel. For Mark, salvation is the restoration of sight by Jesus. In the Purpose of the Parables passage Mark speaks of the blindness of the outsiders, but then goes on to speak of the blindness of the insiders. "Do you not understand this parable? How then will you understand all the parables?" (4:13). The incomprehension of the disciples serves as a warning to "insiders" that those who have been called can also be susceptible to spiritual myopia. Similarly the two-stage healing of a blind man at Bethsaida is closely related to Peter's partial blindness in his confession where the spokesman for the disciples does not fully grasp the heart of the message of salvation. "For the people in Mark's church who also only have spiritual half-sight and have not fully experienced the fruit of redemption, 10:46-52 is of particular importance. Bartimaeus serves as a prototype of the true disciple and provides a model for the Christian who needs to know what it means to see and to be saved. After he receives the gift of sight he follows Jesus on the way."[8]

[8]*Ibid.*, p. 201.

CHAPTER 18
MYSTERY OF THE
KINGDOM AND DISCIPLESHIP

IN MARK THE TEACHING ON DISCIPLESHIP IS concentrated in the second half of the gospel and presented in close conjunction with the passion predictions. But the two halves of the gospel are not watertight compartments. Teaching on discipleship is found also in the first half of the gospel, as in the calling and sending of the disciples. It has even been suggested that the Mystery of the Kingdom given to the insiders (Mark 4) and Discipleship are one and the same thing. The "mystery of the Kingdom of God" is nothing other than Jesus' teaching on discipleship imparted to the disciples in private instruction, which they in turn were to pass on to the Church.

For Wilhelm Wrede the "messianic secret" had to do with the *identity* of Jesus; it was a matter of christology. But it can be argued that the "messianic secret" and the "mystery of the Kingdom of God" cannot be identical. The "mystery" is given to the disciples at 4:12 (The Parable Chapter) and yet it is not until the confession of Peter in 8:29 that any christological affirmation is made. As Schuyler Brown puts it: "The solution, it seems to me, is quite simply that the secret of the kingdom of God, which the disciples are given according to 4:11, is *not* the same as the secret of Jesus' identity, about which they continue to manifest total incomprehension until the break-through in 8:29."[1]

The Secret of the Kingdom

Jesus expresses surprise when the disciples do not understand the parable of the Sower ("Do you not understand this parable?" 4:12), yet the disciples are still distinguished from the uncomprehending mass of people. After that, however, the disciples' incomprehension is viewed more seriously and after the second feeding miracle Jesus administers a stinging rebuke and the disciples are put on a level with the crowds. The incomprehension cannot be concerned with the same thing in the two cases. The way in which the two secrets (discipleship and identity) are revealed to the disciples is different. The secret of the Kingdom of God (discipleship) is revealed by the miraculous cure of the blind man at Bethsaida (8:22-26), which immediately precedes the scene at Caesarea Philippi. Just as the blind man's eyes are opened, so the disciples "see the light" and finally come to realize who Jesus is, at least obscurely. The first secret is revealed by instruction; the second is occasioned by a miracle.

"Our conclusion must be, therefore," writes Schuyler Brown, "that for Mark the incomprehension of the people concerning the meaning of Jesus' parables in ch. 4 (and the disciples' own incomprehension prior to the explanation) is quite distinct from the incomprehension of the disciples concerning who Jesus really is. And, by the same token, the secret of the kingdom of God, which is hidden from the people but revealed to the disciples, and the messianic secret, which even the disciples fail to penetrate until Caesarea Philippi, cannot be taken to be identical. This conclusion can be avoided only by denying any connection between 4:11a and the allegorical interpretation of the para-

---

[1]Schuyler Brown, "The Secret of the Kingdom of God" (Mark 4:11), *Journal of Biblical Literature*, 92(1973), 62.

ble of the sower given by Jesus in 4:14-20."[2]

For Mark "the secret of the Kingdom of God" is no longer what it was for Jesus when he delivered the parable of the Sower—without the allegorical interpretation. The secret no longer has to do with the hidden presence of God's royal rule in Jesus' ministry but rather with the secret instructions which Jesus delivers to his disciples for the benefit of the Christian community. For Mark the secret of the Kingdom of God, unlike the messianic secret formulated in 8:29, is not kerygmatic but didactic. The context of Mark 4 requires that the Mystery be taken to refer to the Interpretation. But the Interpretation is concerned solely with the varied reception of the Word. At this point, of course, we are reaching back into Redaction Criticism.

The Interpretation of the Sower

Mark inserts the saying about imparting the secret to the disciples into the middle of his parable discourse. By doing so he shows us that he understands the parables to refer not simply to Jesus' ministry but the ministry of the disciples as well. The parables are up-dated and made relevant to the situation of the missionary church, an objective which is achieved by the allegorical Interpretation. By way of example the Sower is allegorized into an exhortation both to recent converts (mere reception of the word does not guarantee perseverance) and to the missionaries themselves (those who reject the word or later abandon their faith-commitment will be more than compensated for by the number of faithful, fruitful Christians). The second and third parables could have been interpreted equally well. They lent themselves admirably to the idea of growth of the Christian mission, viewed either as the result of God's silent working (Seed Growing Secretly) or in the light of the disproportion between the humble beginnings and the extraordinary success (Mustard Seed).

[2]*Ibid.*, pp. 62-63.

For Mark the secret of the Kingdom of God means concretely the instruction or exhortation addressed to the Christian community. Significantly Jesus nowhere states in his *public* preaching that the parables concern the Kingdom of God; he does this only when he is alone with the disciples. Having presented the schema public discourse-private explanation in connection with the Sower, Mark can presuppose this schema for the other two parables as well. Private instruction for the disciples figures in four later chapters in Mark and in every instance it concerns a matter of great concern to Christians of the early Church. In Chapter 7 the private instruction treats of ritual cleanness and the Corban and sets forth what defilement means within the Christian community. In Chapter 9 the secret instruction concerns the disciples' activity as exorcists. In Chapter 10, after the discussion about divorce, "in the house the disciples asked him again about this matter" (vs. 10) and Jesus spoke his mind clearly and emphatically. Finally, in the Farewell Discourse (Chapter 13) Jesus takes four disciples aside to a remote spot on the Mount of Olives to give them a secret instruction concerning those things they would have to face when he was no longer with them (persecution, false Christs, and false prophets). Contrary to the authentic proclamation of the nearness of the Kingdom, the latter would proclaim that the Christ is *already* returning (vss. 21-22).

Advice and Encouragement

The parallels between the latter four passages and Mark 4 are not equally strong in all cases. "But what all these passages do have in common is a secret instruction given to the disciples in order to provide advice, consolation, or encouragement, so that they will be able to cope with the problems which will confront them in their future ministry. Another point which is common to all these passages is that none of the instructions which they contain concern the messianic secret, i.e., the mystery of who Jesus is. Their object is not kerygma but didache. We believe that because of the close formal similarities which these parallels exhibit to Mark 4 they provide a more reliable indication of Mark's understanding of the content of the secret of the kingdom of God than do those passages...where Jesus, after having performed miracles which clearly manifest his messianic dignity, chides his disciples for failing to have gotten the point."[3]

In Mark the secrecy motif is connected with both kerygma ("Jesus is the Christ") and didache (the community catechesis, consisting of various instructions and exhortations). The latter is imparted in the form of an interpretation or explanation given privately to the disciples, following upon a parable, enigmatic word, or even action of Jesus. The parables of Mark 4 and the other passages we have examined are didactic parables. The secret of the Kingdom of God refers to secret instruction confined to the circle of the disciples who, in the post-Easter period, will have the responsibility of instructing the community, even as Jesus had instructed them.

The Disciples and Christians

A secret instruction was confided to the circle of disciples who will have the responsibility of instructing the community of Christians. This is already to say that common elements characterize the condition of both disciple and Christian, and included among these elements are mystery and ambiguity, which result in a challenge to faith, and for both disciple and Christian. For the Church in Mark's day (or for ours), as for the contemporaries of Jesus in the narrative, the acknowledgement of Jesus' authority requires faith, for his authority is exercised in words and actions that are in every case ambiguous. In the final and recapitulating set of controversies over Jesus' authority, his contemporaries are challenged to make up their minds on the basis of what they have seen and heard (11:27-33). Mark's readers in

[3]*Ibid.*, p. 70.

their turn will have to make their decision about the significance of Jesus' life.

Part of Mark's practical intent was to declare to his readers that the ambiguities and perplexities and dangers in which they stand are no different from those encountered by the first disciples themselves. This allows or leads him to let the real ambiguity of the historical situation appear right to the end. Jesus' sole word from the cross is, "My God, my God, why hast thou forsaken me?" and the account ends with the well-known reaction of the women to the empty tomb and the word of the "young man": "And they went out and fled from the tomb; for trembling and astonishment had come upon them; and they said nothing to anyone, for they were afraid." "Such resolution of this ambiguity as there is lies outside the Marcan narrative in the conviction of the presence of the Risen Lord with his own in the midst of the ambiguities of their history (cf. 16:7 again), a presence soon to be experienced as that of the Holy Spirit. That, however, belongs not to St. Mark's narrative, but to his life. His narrative is that of 'the *beginning* of the Gospel.' "[4]

The Commission

A number of perspectives borrowed from literary studies help us to read Mark as a unitary narrative. One such perspective is that of the *commission*, task or contract, a common feature of narrative structure. A commission is accepted by a narrative character and this results in a unified narrative sequence as the narrator tells us how the character fulfills that commission or fails to fulfill it. Events of the plot take on meaning because they represent movement toward the goal and obstacles to its realization. In Mark Jesus receives a commission from God (Son of Man, Messiah, Son of God) and the disciples receive a commission from Jesus (discipleship).

An implied author (cf. Chapter 24) often sets out to instill or reinforce certain values and this endeavor provides a clue

[4]Holt Graham, "The Gospel according to St. Mark. Mystery and Ambiguity," *Anglican Theological Review*, Suppl. 7(1976), 45.

to his purpose in writing. Through the narrative he presents a unique vision of goodness and truth for the readers' consideration. Whenever the characters in the narrative act contrary to those values, tension is set up—a tension between the readers' assumption of goodness and truth and the vision presented in the story. Mark's readers are expected to evaluate the disciples' actions in the light of the words and actions of Jesus; the story lines which develop from the commission of Jesus and the commission of the disciples should run parallel. Whenever they do not, a negative judgment of the disciples is demanded by the norms of the narrative. But the story is told for the readers' instruction and correction. The internal tension of the story (between Jesus and disciples) contributes to the external tension (between the implied author's values and those of the implied reader).

Particularly significant is the fact that Mark presents the disciples favorably in the early part of the gospel, making clear the greatness to which they had been called and their initial positive response. But then the signs of incomprehension begin to appear, the disciples are unable to respond because of anxious self-concern. Then Mark depicts the disciples in open conflict with Jesus on issues central to their commission, until finally he shows the disciples breaking faith with Jesus and deserting him at the passion.

The author anticipated, R. Tannehill concludes, "that his readers would identify with the disciples early in the Gospel so that the negative turn in the disciples' story would lead the readers to reexamine their own discipleship. Thus the purpose of the author of Mark was not merely to present certain ideas about Jesus or to warn his readers against some group distinct from themselves but to lead his readers through a particular story in which they could discover themselves and thereby change. If this is true, the tension between Jesus and the disciples, internal to the story, mirrors an external tension between the church as the author perceives it and the discipleship to which it is called."[5]

[5]Robert C. Tannehill, "Tension in Synoptic Sayings and Stories," *Interpretation*, 34(1980), 150.

CHAPTER 19
ENTRY INTO JERUSALEM

IN THE LAST PART OF MARK'S GOSPEL, Chapters 11-16, we have an intricate drama in the course of which the old temple (represented by the leaders of the Jews) is replaced by another temple, "not made with hands," through Jesus' resurrection from the dead. It begins with Jesus' arrival at Jerusalem from Galilee and it ends when the women flee from the empty tomb in silence and fear.

On Palm Sunday Jesus rides into Jerusalem to the acclaim of the people. On this occasion he "went into the temple and looked around at everything," (11:11). The next day Jesus cleanses the temple, declaring that while the temple should have been a place of prayer, it had been turned into a den of robbers. And the account of this incident is bracketed by the cursing of the fig tree. After the second half of the fig tree passage, Jesus tells the parable of the Vineyard, in the course of which he quotes Psalm 118:22, which speaks of rejection and vindication (the stone rejected which becomes the head of the corner).

The remainder of Chapter 12 is another passage devoted to discipleship with a strong emphasis on moral, ethical teaching: taxes, resurrection, the great commandment (Shema), pride and humility, the widow's mite. In the context this passage stands forth as an example of ethics for those to whom the Vineyard is given (the Christian community, the temple was not made with hands). It is in this context of instruction on discipleship that Mark places Jesus' discourse on last things (a farewell discourse). The destruction of the temple is a central topic in this discourse.

The Two Trials

After the Last Supper Jesus is arrested in the garden of Gethsemane and is led to the high priest, "and all the chief priests and the elders and the scribes were assembled." Two charges are laid against Jesus. First, that he said, "I will destroy this temple that is made with hands, and in three days I will build another, not made with hands," (14:58). But it is also said that the testimony of the witnesses was false and that the witnesses did not agree. In the second place, the high priest asked Jesus, "Are you the Christ the Son of the Blessed?" (vs. 61). And Jesus answers: "I am; and you will see the Son of Man seated at the right hand of Power, and coming with the clouds of heaven," (vs. 62). The account of Jesus' trial before the leaders of the Jews is bracketed by the trial of Peter in the courtyard below at the hands of a servant girl, one of the maids of the high priest. While some in the courtroom are striking Jesus and saying to him "Prophesy!" — in the courtyard below, Peter hears the cock crow.

Jesus is led to the place of execution and the inscription of the charge against him reads: "The King of the Jews." As he hung on the cross the chief priests mocked him to one another with the scribes saying: "Let the Christ, the King of the Jews, come down now from the cross," (15:32). "And those who passed by derided him, wagging their heads, and saying, 'Aha! You who would destroy the temple and build it in three days, save yourself, and come down from the cross!'" Then Mark writes that "the curtain of the temple was torn in two, from top to bottom. And when the centurion, who stood facing him, saw that he thus breathed his last, he said, 'Truly this man was the Son of God!'" (vss. 38-39). There is irony in all this. On the deeper level of the story it is those who condemned Jesus who are rejected, while Jesus, the Crucified Messiah, is vindicated and exalted.

The Entry

The note of ambiguity is particularly noticeable in the Entry. Some of the crowd are shouting one thing: others something else. Some people cry out: "Blessed is the kingdom of our father David that is coming!" (11:10), but others exclaim: "Blessed is he who comes in the name of the Lord!" (vs. 9). That is to say, some hail Jesus as the Messiah, others as the eschatological prophet, and in the discussions which follow Jesus expresses his ambiguous relationship to messiahship (12:35-37).

Speculations about Elijah as the eschatological prophet were present in the minds of those who witnessed or wrote about the events described in the New Testament. This is evident from the John the Baptist passages. But, as D. Daube notes in a series of studies on messianic types, such speculation "may account for two incidents not so far associated with him: the way in which Jesus is acclaimed on entering Jerusalem, and the rending of the veil of the temple."[1]

As Jesus is about to enter Jerusalem, the multitude, according to Mark, greets him with the exclamation: "Hosanna! Blessed is he that comes in the name of the Lord!" This is a quotation from the Psalms (118:26). But others in the crowd shout: "Blessed is the kingdom of our father David that is coming! Hosanna in the highest!" This seems to be Mark's interpretation of the greeting or one which he found in his source. The question is whether the evangelists are justified in ascribing a messianic meaning to the greeting, and if so, whether they have given it the right kind of messianic meaning.

In the view of some rabbis, the verse Ps 118:26 together

---

[1] *New Testament and Rabbinic Judaism*, p. 20.

with a few that precede and follow were messianic. It was believed that they were composed when David became king and would be recited again when the Messiah appears. This exegesis definitely existed by the first half of the third century A.D., but we cannot say for sure whether it goes back to the first. One point, however, is suggestive. There is remarkable similarity between the way the rabbis used Psalm 118 and the way it is quoted in Mark. The rabbis put several lines, not just "Blessed is he" etc., into the mouth of the public welcoming David or the Messiah. When the Messiah appears, the people inside Jerusalem will say, "Hosanna," those outside, "O Lord, send prosperity"; those inside, "Blessed is he that comes in the name of the Lord," those outside, "We bless you of the house of the Lord." The crowd welcoming Jesus combines at least two of these verses: "Blessed is he" and "Hosanna."

The One to Come

On the other hand, in the prophet Malachi we read: "Behold, I send my messenger (*malachi*) to prepare the way before me, and the Lord will suddenly come to his temple; the messenger of the covenant in whom you delight," (3:1). And in the last verses of the same chapter this messenger is identified with Elijah and thereby Elijah became the eschatological prophet. This latter passage becomes important when viewed in the context of the rite of circumcision. All over the world, the circumcision of a Jewish boy, Daube writes, "begins by the boy being brought into a room where the participants in the service are already assembled, and the latter exclaiming, 'Blessed is he that cometh, *barukh haba*'."[2]

The words may be addressed to the angel Elijah accompanying the boy or to the boy as Elijah: in either case they are addressed to Elijah. As Malachi announced of the "messenger of the covenant," "Behold he comes," it was natural

[2]*Ibid.*, p. 22.

for the rabbis to connect the verse "Blessed is he that comes in the name of the Lord," with Elijah, the same person in their eyes. Quite apart from the circumcision service, this was as appropriate a greeting for Elijah as for the Messiah himself. Elijah is introduced as "the coming one" in several synoptic pericopes.

The greeting of Jesus by the multitude was of a messianic character, but both the eschatological prophet and the messiah were messianic characters. Some of the crowd seems to have been hailing the one, some the other. Exactly which messianic figure the crowd had in mind is not clear; it may have been the son of David, the king of Israel, but it may also have been Elijah.

In contrast to the other evangelists, Mark carefully avoids making the messianic character of the incident fully explicit. The sending for the colt is set forth without explanation, apparently as a plain narrative of history; Zechariah is not quoted or referred to (contrast Mt 21:5 and John 12:15); the ovation comes not from a multitude, but simply from the little band with Jesus, and some were hailing the Messiah, others the Eschatological Prophet.

At one time this ambiguity would have been marked down to the theory of a "messianic secret." It seems more likely that the ambiguity was inherent in the event itself and that Mark simply lets it appear (in his own way) in a gospel written for those who are themselves in the ambiguous position of professing faith in a Messiah and Lord who was crucified, and that at the risk of martyrdom. As in the Entry, so in what follows, the participants in the drama and any who (in Mark's day) hold too fast to traditional forms of expectation are met with ambiguity and confounded.

The title "Messiah" is ascribed to Jesus in 1:1 but this benefits only the reader; specific messianic and royal images are almost totally absent from the accounts of Jesus' ministry in the gospels. It is in the passion story that Jesus is portrayed as a king, the Messiah-King. It is paradoxical that such imagery suddenly becomes prominent precisely at the stage in the story at which Jesus looks least like the traditional Messiah.

The Crucified Messiah

The explanation would seem to be that the title Messiah came to be inextricably bound up with the name of Jesus precisely because Jesus was actually crucified as the Messiah. Actually it is very strange that precisely the title Messiah was applied to Jesus and became his name. The title stems from that figure in Jewish eschatology that has almost nothing at all in common with the New Testament picture of Christ. The "Messiah," used absolutely as an eschatological term, designates the political Messiah, the king of the house of David. That Christian believers added the title Messiah to Jesus' name because of later theologizing seems unlikely. The true explanation seems to be that "if Jesus was executed as a would-be king, then, for his followers, his resurrection by God was a vindication; he was the risen King (Messiah-King, for the Jews)."[3]

Jesus' enemies had been wrong about him. He died as King, and God vindicated him by raising him from the dead, therefore he was vindicated as King. It follows that he is the Crucified and Risen Messiah. Despite the radically unconventional nature of Jesus' messiahship the image of Jesus as Messiah sticks in Christian tradition because of the turn of events during his last days in Jerusalem and because of the centrality of his death and resurrection in Christian preaching.

Early Christians were convinced that Jesus was the Messiah promised in the Scriptures; that he fulfilled the traditional messianic texts (Isa 11; 2 Sam 7:10-14; Ps 2). But the early Christians did not limit themselves to the traditional messianic passages. In light of Jesus' unique ministry, they redefined messiahship, omitting much of the traditional imagery (because Jesus did not appear as a warrior-king) and made use of other, previously non-messianic texts. Most radical of all in the eyes of their fellow Jews, Christians insisted that the highest messianic action was Jesus'

[3]D. Juel, *Introduction to New Testament Literature*, p. 156.

death and they assembled passages that were not tradition-
ally viewed in Jewish circles as descriptions of the coming
Messiah-King to prove the messianic nature of Jesus' death.
Jesus is the Crucified Messiah.

Mark does not include the title Son of Man within the
circle of such titles as Messiah, King, Son of David, and Son
of God. While he places the latter titles in apposition to one
another, he never places Messiah and Son of Man in apposition to each other. Further, Jesus is never confessed to be
the Son of Man or even addressed as such. Yet there is no
aura of secrecy surrounding the title; Jesus calls himself the
Son of Man in the full hearing of the scribes and Pharisees.

A strong note of opposition characterizes the title Son of
Man. Jesus designates himself as the Son of Man in scenes
in which his enemies take offense at the authority with
which he acts and in his passion predictions. Yet in the
parousia passages Jesus designates himself as the Son of
Man as he prophesies his vindication before the world. He
will come at the end of time as Judge and inaugurate God's
consummated Kingdom.

This explains how the trial scene is to be understood. The
high priest asks Jesus whether he is "the Messiah, the Son of
the Blessed," (14:61). Jesus replies, "I am!" then goes on to
say, "and you will see the Son of Man sitting on the right
hand of power and coming with the clouds of heaven." "The
sense of Jesus' words is this: Inasmuch as you have asked me
whether I am the Son of God in order to condemn me, it will
be as your Judge that you will see the Son of Man coming in
glory at the latter day (cf. 14:55; 8:38)."[4]

[4]J. D. Kingsbury, *Interpretation*, 35(1981), 257.

CHAPTER 20
CLEANSING OF THE TEMPLE

IN CHAPTERS 11-16 WE WITNESS an intricate drama in the course of which the old temple (represented by the leaders of the Jews) is replaced by another temple, "not made with hands" (the Christian community) through Jesus' resurrection from the dead. It begins with Jesus' arrival at Jerusalem from Galilee and it ends when the women flee from the empty tomb in silence and fear.

On Palm Sunday Jesus rides into Jerusalem to the acclaim of the people, an acclamation drawn from Ps 118:26. The ambiguous nature of the messianic acclamation on this occasion has a lesson for Mark's readers who have professed allegiance to an even more ambiguous figure, a Crucified Messiah. After the Entry Jesus "went into the temple and looked around at everything," (11:11). The next day Jesus cleanses the temple, declaring that while the temple should have been a place of prayer, it had been turned into "a den of robbers." The latter quotation, from Jeremiah 7:11, takes on great meaning when it is brought into conjunction with the Abomination of Desolation of the Farewell Discourse, Mark 13, which we shall consider later. And the account of this incident is bracketed by the cursing of the fig tree. After the second half of the fig tree passage, Jesus tells the parable of the Vineyard, in the course of which he quotes Ps 118:22, which speaks of rejection and vindication (the stone rejected which becomes the head of the corner).

The Cursing and the Cleansing

The Cleansing of the Temple, framed by the Cursing of the Fig Tree, is one of Mark's most effective brackets—one that rivals the Trials of Jesus and Peter in dramatic effectiveness. The bracket or frame is a method of creating narrative. By Mark's time the time had come for the individual gospel traditions to be placed under the control of an overall interpretation of the career of Jesus of Nazareth. For that a narrative framework was necessary, within which those traditions could be used in the service of that larger interpretation. Mark shaped traditions themselves so that they could function as part of his longer story, he placed individual stories in special arrangements, and he composed short summaries and interpretative comments, which he then placed at strategic points in his narrative. And in doing this Mark made use of the amalgam of drama, rhetoric, and history, and the resulting concentric development which characterized his age.

By juxtaposing traditions to one another, Mark was able to allow them to interpret each other in such a way that made further comment unnecessary in many cases. Much of what he wanted to say, he said by means of the way he ordered the traditions at his disposal. One must pay careful attention to Mark's arrangement of those earlier traditions. Such arrangements and juxtapositions constitute a major hermeneutical device.

Among the events Mark narrates during Jesus' final visit to Jerusalem are the Cleansing of the Temple and the Cursing of a Fig Tree (11:12-25). Mark has taken the account of the Cleansing and bracketed it with the story of the Cursing, and in that way clearly indicating that he intends the two stories to be understood in relationship to each other. In this way he makes a point he wants to emphasize about the importance of Jesus over against the historic importance of temple worship within Jewish religious life.

"For All Nations..."

The Cleansing took place in the outermost of the three courtyards surrounding the temple, the Court of the Gentiles. For convenience sake the temple authorities allowed the sacrificial animals to be sold there and the coins of the pilgrims to be exchanged for the Tyrian coinage, in which alone the annual tribute to the temple and payments for the sacrificial traffic could be made. This arrangement was of the greatest assistance to the Jewish pilgrims from both near and far, though it also may no doubt have been a source of profit to the temple authorities. As regards the interior parts of the temple, devoted to Jewish sacrifice and Jewish worship, Jesus at this point did not intervene directly. On the other hand he appears to charge the authorities with the desecration of the whole building owing to the traffic which they permitted in this outer court.

In support of his action Jesus quotes Isaiah: "My house shall be called a house of prayer *for all nations*," (56:7). It is significant that of the synoptic writers Mark alone quotes the last three words, "for all nations." Isaiah was speaking of a future reality. According to Isaiah the Jewish temple would one day, when the messianic age arrived, become a house of prayer not only for the Jews but for all the nations. Taken apart from the bracket, both Jesus' action and prophecy are concerned with the rights and privileges of Gentiles. No direct attempt is made to interfere with the existing Jewish ritual or worship, and Jesus confines himself entirely to the removal, from the Court of the Gentiles, of all that made prayer and worship difficult or impossible for Gentiles, in that one and only part of the temple to which they had already the privilege of access.

Much exclusivism is met with in the Old Testament, but from time to time universalism is also introduced (Second Isaiah, Jonah). Universalism may not have been prominent in Jewish thought in Jesus' time, so the meaning of Jesus' action was not immediately apparent. But in the messianic context of Jesus' mission the Cleansing assumes a momentous character. Even before the arrival of the messianic king the Gentiles had been allowed certain privileges upon the threshold of the temple, and of these the Jewish authorities had allowed them to be robbed. "Must it not therefore be the first act of the messianic king on his arrival to restore to Gentiles at least those religious rights and privileges which ought already to be theirs, especially if, as would surely happen with the coming of the Messiah, Jewish worship would now become a univeral worship?"[1] In Jesus' action therefore we see him concerned with the position of the Gentile nations in respect of their worship of the one true God.

Jesus' public ministry, as a whole, was directed to the Jews. It is Jesus' death and resurrection that is to change the status of Gentiles in relation to Jews. In Matthew on the occasion of the mission of the Twelve, we find the injunction: "Go nowhere among the Gentiles," (10:5). But in the last words of Matthew's gospel the disciples are expressly bidden to evangelize "all the nations," the very expression used in the quotation from Isaiah in Mark, on the occasion of the Cleansing. For the same reason Matthew omits the phrase in connection with the Cleansing. Matthew wishes to bring out as clearly as possible that it is the Lord's atoning death and resurrection which renders possible the universalism of his work and message.

The Cleansing also was ambiguous. Universalism was not prominent and Jesus' actions affected directly only the outer courtyard. Yet the Cleansing is also a sign or token that with Jesus' arrival at Jerusalem the messianic age was at the door. Consequently Jesus' action was also concerned, even if only indirectly, with the Jewish ordinances. For these, though no doubt the Lord's gifts to the people of his choice, were ordained, like all things Jewish, for the period *preceding* the end or consummation. The Cleansing was a prophetic sign that the Lord's house was a house of prayer for all peoples.

The clue to the passage is in vs. 17, where Mark, alone

---

[1]R. H. Lightfoot, *Gospel Message*, pp. 64-65.

among the Evangelists, completes the quotation from Isaiah by including the words *for all the nations*. The attack on the money-changers and the merchants is far more important than simply an indication of Jesus' displeasure at such activity within the temple precincts. Above all, Jesus' attack is not an expression of his indignation at dishonest business practices; there seems to be no reference at all to this in the text. The Jews allowed trading in the court of the Gentiles, and by so doing they were robbing the Gentiles even of such privileges on the threshold of the temple as had been granted to them. The first act of the messianic king on his arrival at the temple must be to restore to the Gentiles their religious rights, for with his coming the prophecy would be fulfilled and Jewish worship would become the universal worship. Jesus' action is the fulfillment of a further aspect of the messianic role, that of vindicating the Gentiles and gathering them into the life and worship of the people of God.

Den of Robbers

But the broader implications of the Cleansing must also be taken into consideration. While the cleansing took place in the court of the Gentiles, what Jesus did there had implications for temple worship as a whole. "By an act of prophetic protest, Jesus demonstrated that the practices necessary for the normal functioning of the temple must come to an end. If sacrificial animals cannot be purchased, then the sacrifice cannot be carried on. If money proper for the paying of the half-sheckel temple tax cannot be obtained, the monetary support of the temple and its priesthood would have to come to an end."[2]

The temple has become a "den of robbers" not because dishonest practices were carried on there but because (as we shall see in connection with the Farewell Discourse) it was used as a place of retreat after the robbers have committed their crimes elsewhere. Jesus' protest is directed against the

[2]Paul J. Achtemeier, *Mark*, (Philadelphia: Fortress Press, 1975), p. 24.

use to which the temple was being put. People were thinking that so long as the temple services are continued, they may retreat there, no matter how they have acted outside its walls, and still find forgiveness and fellowship with God.

The Cleansing represents Jesus' prophetic-symbolic act of ending cultic worship within the temple, because it has been abused on the assumption that the temple cult made forgiveness for any kind of behavior automatic, and because the necessary universal worship of God, to be centered in the temple, simply had not come about. The effectiveness of the Cursing of the Fig Tree, noted after the Cleansing, makes clear that the temple, too, will ultimately be destroyed. With Jesus' death, the temple is symbolically destroyed (tearing the veil, 15:38) as it will finally be physically destroyed in A.D. 70 by the Romans.

Two features in the Isaiah quote seem particularly appropriate in Mark writing for Christians—the reference to the "house of prayer" and the reference to "all the nations." There is a subtle concern for Gentiles in Mark. In the Farewell Discourse Jesus declares that "the gospel must first be preached to all nations," (13:10). The first to make a true confession after Jesus' death is a Gentile, the Roman centurion. The quotation from Isaiah seems well chosen. The verse is part of a promise to the eunuch and the foreigner who have kept justice, done righteousness and kept the Sabbath (vs. 2), that they will have a share in the promises soon to be fulfilled for God's people. They too will have a place on God's holy mountain; their sacrifices too will be accepted (vs. 7). The verse quoted in Mark is the concluding promise explaining God's final purpose: "For my house shall be called a house of prayer for all peoples," (Isa 56:7).

House of Prayer

The other aspect of the Isaiah quote requiring attention is the reference to the "house of prayer." The phrase is attested elsewhere as a name for the temple; it need not imply an opposition to the sacrificial cult and certainly does not in the text of Isaiah. But there are other indications that Mark does oppose the sacrificial cult. The parable of the Vineyard is followed by another ethical passage (ethics for the new people to whom the Vineyard would be given). There it is declared that the twin commandment, love of God and neighbor, is much more than all whole burnt offerings and sacrifices (12:33). Some opposition between "house of prayer" and sacrificial cult does not seem inconceivable in Mark. The temple is not the house of prayer for all nations God intended, but instead a "den of robbers." The present order will be cursed like the fig tree; the vineyard will be given to others. The temple will be destroyed (Farewell Address, Temple Veil), to be replaced by a new reality (a "temple not made with hands," 14:58).

Whatever its original meaning in Christian tradition, the Fig Tree Bracket provides an insight into the meaning of the Cleansing. The story is narrated not simply to display Jesus' miraculous power nor simply to introduce the saying on prayer, even if this is the function of the pericope with respect to form. In vs. 14 we read that Jesus said to the tree, "'May no one ever eat fruit from you again.' And his disciples heard" (*ekouon*, impf., "they were hearing"). The use of the imperfect helps extend the action into the Cleansing, to be picked up again in the second half of the bracket ("And Peter remembered and said to him" vs.21). Mark intends the reader to keep the story of the fig tree in mind while reading the story of the cleansing.

The Cleansing must in some sense imply the rejection of the official representatives of Israel, the leaders of the temple establishment. It is especially to be noted, however, that Jesus' opponents in the last chapters of the gospel are clearly the leaders of the temple establishment, "the scribes, the high priests, and the elders." The Cleansing, interpreted by the Cursing of the Fig Tree, points to the rejection of a particular group within Israel, not of Israel as a whole. Those in charge of the temple have borne no fruit; they will be rejected.

This position seems to be confirmed by the contents of the second part of the Fig Tree Bracket. It ends with observations on prayer ("Whatever you ask, it will be yours," vs. 24) and forgiveness ("Forgive that your Father may forgive," vs. 26). The juxtaposition of the saying on prayer with a story whose point seems to be that the temple establishment will be rejected because it has not made the temple into a "house of prayer for all nations" seems to result from careful arrangement. "The saying on prayer is clearly intended for Mark's church. Perhaps Mark wishes to characterize the community of the faithful as a community typified by prayer and forgiveness. The contrast between the praying community and the 'house of prayer' that has become a 'den of robbers' already suggests that the distinction between a 'temple made with hands' and a 'temple not made with hands' in 14:58 may reflect the author's view of the Christian community as a replacement of the rejected temple establishment."[3]

The Cleansing, with its reference to a "house of prayer" is appropriately followed by further sayings on prayer and forgiveness (11:20-26), and then, in Chapter 12, by the parable of the Vineyard which underlines the idea of taking the Kingdom from those who then held it and giving it to others. Then, in the rest of Chapter 12, there follows further ethical instruction such as would be appropriate for the new holders of the Kingdom.

[3]Donald Juel, *Messiah and Temple*, (Missoula: Scholars Press, 1977), pp. 135-36.

CHAPTER 21
THE FAREWELL ADDRESS, MARK 13

WE HAVE SEEN MARK BUILDING UP a strong context of rejection and vindication. The Cleansing, interpreted by the Cursing of the Fig Tree, points to the rejection of a particular group within Israel. In the Cleansing the theme of the rejection of the Jewish leaders is linked with the impending destruction of the temple by the reference to Jeremiah 7:11: "You have made the temple a den of robbers." This interpretation is confirmed by the Parable of the Vineyard, which intimates that the Jewish religious leaders, the tenants, will be destroyed and their "vineyard" given to others. This is followed by negative statements about sacrifice (12:32-34). In this context Jesus explicitly predicts the destruction of the temple complex at the beginning of the Farewell Discourse (13:1-2). Finally, at the moment of Jesus' death, the temple veil is torn from top to bottom.

A Farewell Discourse

Recent years have witnessed a growing conviction that Mark 13 is not an apocalypse, as was believed for so long, but a farewell discourse of the type found in Deut 32 and

John 14-17, the Last Supper Discourse. This latter discourse exemplifies a pattern well established in the Old Testament: the farewell speech delivered by a famous man before death. Such farewell speeches appear already in the earliest books of the Old Testament: Jacob's farewell and blessings to his children in Genesis, Joshua's farewell to Israel in Joshua. Indeed, the whole book of Deuteronomy is made up of Moses' farewell speeches to Israel. Tobit's death-bed farewell to Tobias comes from late Old Testament times when the form became even more popular. In the New Testament Paul's speech to the elders of Ephesus is a type of farewell speech. "The common situation is that of a great man who gathers together his followers (his children, his disciples, or the people) on the eve of his death to give them the instructions that will help them after his departure. In John this occurs in the setting of a final meal."[1]

The themes and methods of composition found in Moses' farewell speech (Deut 32) are similar to the themes and methods of composition which we find in Mark 13. Deuteronomy 32 resonates with a number of motifs found also in Mark 13. Despite the trials, tribulations, and natural catastrophes of the present moment the author reassures his readers that God will intervene on the part of his people and thus they will be saved. In terms of the composition, both texts consist of Old Testament texts that are combined in rabbinic exegetical fashion to portray events which the author envisions as the final manifestations of God's purpose.

Concentric development is important for an understanding of Mark 13. While the original question centers upon the destruction of the temple, the concentric development suggests that this has already happened and that Mark's readers should henceforth fix their gaze on the only events worth awaiting: the end of the world and the coming of the Son of Man.

---

[1]Raymond E. Brown, *The Gospel according to John*, (xiii-xxi), (Garden City: Doubleday, 1970), p. 598.

As usual the discourse divides into three parts. In Part 1, vss. 5-23, Christological elements (coming of the Son of Man) frame events of destruction. In Part 2, these two elements are united. Part 3 repeats the pattern of Part 1. The discourse of Mark 13 is a reply to a question ("When will this be, and what will be the sign?" vs. 4). This relates essentially to the event of total destruction which Jesus has just announced (vs. 2), an event which involves the temple. Yet the formulation in both vs. 2 and vs. 4 is sufficiently general to involve the end of time equally well.

Stay Awake!

In the light of this opening, Jesus' reply is unusual. As Mark presents it, Jesus introduces a new perspective, a Christological perspective, absent from the initial question. And the literary structure of the discourse shifts the point of gravity from the destruction of the temple to the cosmic end and the Christological event, the Son of Man's coming in glory (vss. 24-27). All the exhortation which runs through the discourse from one and to the other is an appeal for vigilance for this decisive and final moment. This helps to clarify the meaning of the discourse and gives us an insight into the relationship between the question (vs. 4) and the reply, on the one hand, and the relationship between the text and Mark's readers, on the other.

The question (vs. 4) speaks of a sign which will indicate the moment when "these things are all to be accomplished." In Part 1 we find the sequence of two phrases: "when you will hear," (vs. 7); and "when you will see," (vs. 14). For the former it is clearly indicated that it is not to be brought into relationship with the end (vs. 7). The second is marked by the imminent proximity of the end. This immediacy is discernible already in the verb *see* (vs. 14, "when you will see" the *bdelugma*, as compared with *hear* in vs. 7). The idea of a *sign* which announces the moment of the end (vs. 4), also follows more from sight than from hearing, and the way in which the *bdelugma* is spoken of, citing Daniel and followed by the order "let the reader understand," invites us to regard this passage as the sign which the initial question seeks to know. But the chronological notices which introduce the events of the end of time throw these events into the future ("in those days, after this trial," vs. 24; "and then," vss. 26-27), while the events recounted just before (vss. 19-23) are not thrown into the future.

In order that this relationship of immediacy, seen at vs. 24, be respected on the level of the communication between Mark and his readers, it is necessary that these latter recognize themselves and events of their time in everything that characterizes "those days," (vss. 14-23). This recognition is almost obligatory at vs. 14: "Let the reader understand!" Thus we are led by reasons at once logical and literary to conclude that the events spoken of in vss. 14-23 involve the present and the recent past of the readers of the gospel.

In Part 3 the idea of immediacy reappears: "Truly, I say to you, this generation will not pass away before all these things take place," (vs. 30). Thus for the readers as for the evangelist the sign on which the question of the disciples bears (vs. 4), is behind them and expectation henceforth concerns directly the absolute end: that where everything passes away—"both the heaven and the earth" (vs. 31)—and where the Son of Man appears in glory and power, gathering the elect (vss. 26-27).

Hence Mark's arrangement: everything which concerns the temple, its destruction and/or profanation, is already past, and henceforth the reader's gaze must be fixed on the only events worth awaiting: the end of the world and the coming of the Son of Man.

What Lies Ahead

Mark 13 is a necessary link in the development of thought in Chapters 11-16. From the Entry on, Mark focuses on the temple. When Jesus went into the temple and looked round at everything, "it was already late," (11:11). Time was running out for the old order. The Cleansing, bracketed by the

Cursing, indicates that Jesus' action is in some sense a cursing of the temple order. By the end of Chapter 12 the conflict between Jesus and the temple establishment has risen to a peak. Chapter 13, with Jesus' words about the destruction of the temple, follows upon and forms the climax to the conflict brewing between the temple establishment and Jesus. The prophecy in 13:2 suggests that the destruction of the temple serves as God's confirmation of the charges against the temple establishment and therefore vindicates Jesus against his opponents.

And the theme of conflict extends into the following trial and execution. Jesus is charged with having said that he would destroy the temple; he is taunted with the same charge as he hangs on the cross; and at the moment of his death the temple veil is torn from top to bottom, a portent of the actual destruction to come.

R. H. Lightfoot was already aware of Mark 13 as a Farewell Discourse and he underlined how closely Mark 13 is bound up with its context. In particular Lightfoot saw a close connection between the Farewell Discourse (Chapter 13) and the account of the Passion which follows (Chapters 14-15). Three connecting links are particularly worthy of mention: the verb "to hand over, deliver up" (*paradidomi*); the Son of Man title; and vigilance, the verb "to watch" (*gregoreite*).

Being Handed Over

The term *paradidomi* is used throughout Mark's gospel at certain key moments in the story. At Mark 1:14 it is reported that "after John was handed over, Jesus came into Galilee, preaching the gospel of God." The term is used in two of Mark's three passion predictions (9:31; 10:33). In the Farewell it is affirmed that Jesus' disciples will be handed over to stand trial for their faith in Jesus, "for my sake," (13:9). In the Garden Jesus makes the announcement, "The hour has come; the Son of Man is handed over into the hands of sinners," (14:41). The Sanhedrin hands Jesus over to Pilate

(15:1). And finally Jesus is handed over in order that he might be crucified. Clearly, the use of the term advances the plot of Mark's story to its climactic end. The passion predictions serve to prepare the reader for the fate that awaits Jesus. As Jesus had foretold, the passion narrative progresses toward Jesus' death through the stages of his being handed over by Judas, by the Sanhedrin to Pilate, and finally by Pilate, in order that he might be crucified. What then is the relationship between Jesus' being handed over and the disciples' (the readers of the gospel) being handed over?

The comparison demonstrates that as it goes with Christ, so will it go with those who belong to Christ. Their fates are one. As Jesus was handed over, so the community will also experience the same "for his sake." And it is not merely blind fate that brings Jesus and the community to this end. If the community links its experience to that of Jesus, it will understand that it too goes this way because it is the purpose of God. And if Jesus is vindicated so they shall be also.

Son of Man

In the Farewell Jesus warns against false Christs and then declares: "They will see the Son of Man coming in clouds with great power and glory," (13:26). At the Trial, when asked by the high priest, "Are you the Christ?" Jesus replies: "You will see the Son of Man seated at the right hand of Power, and coming with the clouds of heaven," (14:62). In both these passages we find the Son of Man paired with the title Christ.

And there was an even earlier instance of the same thing, in connection with Peter's confession. After Peter had affirmed, "You are the Christ," Jesus sets out to correct his concept of messiahship, and by the use of the title "Son of Man," Jesus began to teach them, "It is necessary that the Son of Man suffer many things and be killed," (8:31). Mark's point seems to be that Peter "understands yet does not understand." There was no place for suffering and defeat in Peter's concept of messiahship. But his misunderstanding does not necessarily mean that his confession was false, nor does Jesus' characterization of him as Satan have that meaning. His is a half-blind confession, as suggested by the cure of the blindman at Bethsaida just before the Confession scene. Peter does not yet understand the character of Jesus' messiahship. Popular messianic expectations and the image of Jesus as the Crucified Messiah were in conflict. So after Peter recognizes him as Messiah, Jesus goes on to speak of the Son of Man. The Son of Man title is used to develop a redefinition of the popular idea of Messiah in light of Jesus' passion and death.

In the Farewell Jesus declares: "They will see the Son of Man coming in clouds with great power and glory," and at his trial he declares: "You will see the Son of Man seated at the right hand of power, and coming with the clouds of heaven." The Son of Man sayings had served to correct the popular view of the Messiah by bringing it into focus in terms of Jesus' passion and death. In the same way the Son of Man sayings in the Farewell and Trial function to inform the reader that Jesus' death as Messiah will be vindicated when he returns in power and glory. Two days before the Passover Jesus is "anointed for burying" (14:8) and then he shares the Passover meal with his disciples.

"Watch therefore..."

The third connecting link between Farewell and Passion are admonitions "to watch." The Farewell ends with the admonition: "Watch therefore—for you do not know when the master of the house will come, in the evening, or at midnight, or at cockcrow, or in the morning—lest he come suddenly and find you asleep (*katheudontas*). And what I say to you I say to all: Watch," (13:35-37). When they had gone out to the Mount of Olives Jesus instructs the disciples to keep watch (*gregoreita*) while he goes a little farther to pray. And coming (three times) he finds them sleeping (*katheudontas*). The third time he exclaims: "Are you still sleeping and taking your rest? It doesn't matter. The hour has come. Behold the Son of Man is betrayed into the hands of sinners!" (14:41). The very same disciples to whom Jesus had earlier given instruction in the Farewell Discourse (with the exception of Andrew) accompany Jesus to the Garden of Gethsemane. The question is put to the Christian reader: are you doing any better?

There is a pointed contrast between Jesus' agonized recognition of the will of God and the unsuspecting sleep of the disciples who, because they were not watching, did not know that *the hour* had come. "For the Church of Mark's day the example of Jesus in the Garden, as contrasted with the behavior of the three disciples, must have had special value as setting forth the spirit in which the vocation to martyrdom should be approached. The Christian witness must ever be mindful also of the weakness of the flesh."[2] He must *watch* and *pray*, lest he break down when the hour of trial comes. Had Peter and the rest kept vigil in the Garden, they might have stood firm instead of fleeing when Jesus was arrested. Three times Peter is found asleep in the Garden, and subsequently he denies Jesus three times.

Against this background of appeals for vigilance we may ask about another element at the end of the Farewell Discourse—the fourfold chronological indication in vs. 35: "Watch therefore—for you do not know when the master of the house will come, in the evening, or at midnight, or at cockcrow, or in the morning." To divide the night into four watches was a Roman usage, of military origin. Usually the numerical adjective was used: first, second (cf. Mk 6:48, "about the fourth watch of the night").

The terms used by Mark are popular equivalents. But why list all four parts of the night? Granted the correspondence between the end of Mark 13 and the scene in Gethsemane, it seems likely that the four stages indicated in 13:35b are related to a fourfold articulation discernible in the passion account. The vigilance demanded of the disci-

---

[2]A. E. J. Rawlinson, *St. Mark*, (London: Methuen, 1925), p. 211.

ples in Mark 13, with the four points of the night specified, may be understood in connection with the sequence of events of the night before the passion. On that *evening* Jesus *comes* for the Last Supper with the twelve; the scene in Gethsemane and the arrest would take place towards *midnight*; Peter denies the Lord at *cockcrow*; and *in the morning* the chief priests, the elders, and the scribes hold a consultation. "In any case, it is very noticeable that in the Passion narrative of this gospel the last hours of the Lord's life are reckoned at three-hour intervals, which is also the method adopted in 13:35—an exactness of temporal reckoning to which St. Mark is usually indeed a stranger."[3]

Mark 13 is therefore well anchored by its introduction (vss. 1-5) and by its conclusion (vss. 33-37) in the composition of the denouement, the last great part of the gospel. The denouement contains three large sections yet constitutes a single organic unit, which in turn is well integrated into Mark's overall gospel plan. This unity is further enhanced by the way in which the finale of the first section (Chapters 11-12) prepares for the Farewell Discourse and even anticipates the passion account. As Jesus' presence in the temple was coming to an end, just before the great discourse of Mark 13, the short episode of the poor widow (12:41-44) both prepares for the discourse which follows, and points forward to the passion account.

The Two Women

Jesus, surrounded by his disciples (12:43), "sat down opposite the treasury," (vs. 41); the situation is comparable to that sketched in 13:3: "and as he sat...opposite the temple, Peter and James and John and Andrew asked him privately." The story of the poor widow orients us more to the passion (Chs 14-15) than to the coming in glory of the Son of Man (Ch 13). The poor widow is cited as an example for the disciples because of the gift she made of all she

[3]R. H. Lightfoot, *Gospel Message*, p. 53.

possessed, "her whole living," RSV, but literally, *her whole life* (*holon ton bion*, vs. 44). The emphasis obtained by the expression *holon ton bion*, arises from the redundance of these last words in relation to "all she possessed." The widow thus becomes a figure of "the one who came to give his life," (10:45) and it announces the gift that Jesus will make of his own life, recounted in Chs 14-15. Thus the story of the poor widow is linked in a subtle way with the third section of the denouement, the passion account.

When the story resumes, after Mark 13, the chronological note ("two days before the Passover") establishes a link both with what follows and with what goes before. The "chief priests and the scribes" reappear. Their intention to arrest Jesus is repeated and made more explicit; in 14:2 the narrator uses direct address.

The anointing at Bethany (14:3-9) is explicitly brought into relationship with the burial to come (vs. 8). The gesture of the woman of Bethany is linked with that of the poor widow at the entrance to the temple (12:41-44), and also forms an inclusion with the end of the section, where the women are the witnesses of the burial (15:42-47) and set out to embalm the body on the day after the Sabbath (16:1-2).

Both anonymous, these women are cited as an example by Jesus for his disciples, and indirectly for the community. In both instances it is a question of wealth and poverty, and in Jesus' words we see a form of Jesus' identification with the poor. As the poor widow, by offering all she had, announces the passion, so the gesture of the woman of Bethany, anticipating the burial, is brought into relation with the good news of the resurrection.

After the anointing at Bethany preparations are made for the celebration of the Passover. Jesus and his disciples enter the upper room "when evening had come" (*kai opsias genomenes*, 14:17), where Jesus makes the symbolic offering of his body and of his blood shed for many. The same phrase (*kai opsias genomenes*) appears again (15:42) when Jesus is placed in the tomb. Thus, as in classic tragedy, the whole drama of the passion is confined between two sunsets, i.e., in the interval of a day according to Jewish reckoning.

CHAPTER 22

THE ABOMINATION OF DESOLATION

ONE VERSE OF THE FAREWELL DISCOURSE, 13:14, has probably occasioned more speculation than any other verse in the New Testament. "When you see the Abomination of Desolation (*to bdelugma tes eremoseos*) set up where it ought not to be (let the reader understand), then let those who are in Judea flee to the mountains."

The procedure that interpreters have usually followed is to note that the phrase is derived from the book of Daniel. There it referred to the altar of Olympious Zeus that was set up in the Jewish temple by the Syrian King, Antiochus IV Epiphanes (about 146 B.C.). This event is viewed in Daniel as a sign of the end times. The introduction of a pagan idol into the temple would of course imply that the temple had been defiled and was no longer suitable for worship and sacrifice. It has also been argued that the same phrase was used to refer to the image of Caesar that P. Petronius was ordered to erect in the temple in A.D. 40 but which was prevented by the murder of Caligula.

Interpreters then begin their speculations as to what the phrase might have meant in Mark's sources, or on the lips of Jesus, and they come up with various inconclusive answers.

Because it is the only reference to the temple in the body of
the speech it must in some way be related to the prophecy of
destruction in vs. 2. So the Abomination is taken as a
portent of the future, or past, destruction of the temple. But
all the while millenarists continue to identify the Abomination with the scoundrels and villains and other misfortunes
that have appeared down through the ages.

A Literary Approach

This uncertainty reveals the weakness of attempting to
establish the meaning of the Abomination by reference
either to Mark's sources or to the political situation of his
community. Here, perhaps as clearly as anywhere, the
advantages of the literary approach become manifest. The
Abomination must first be understood within the literary
framework of Mark's gospel. "Only then is it appropriate to
hazard a conjecture of the historical associations that
Mark's readers might have made on the basis of *to bdelugma tes eremoseos.* Likewise only after the literary meaning has been established is it appropriate to inquire of the
relationship between Mark's meaning and the meaning that
the phrase might have had in Mark's sources."[1]

What the Abomination meant in the sources is not
dependent upon Mark's use of the phrase; its meaning in the
source could be examined independently of Mark. But it
may well have been that Mark did not adhere rigidly to that
earlier meaning. Therefore, we are on the safest ground
when we inquire of the meaning of *to bdelugma tes eremoseos* on the basis of what can be understood from the literary
context of Mark's gospel.

In our last chapter we observed a number of connecting
links between the Farewell and the Passion. Now we should
take note of a link which connects backwards as it were from
Farewell to Cleansing. After his entry into Jerusalem on
Palm Sunday, Jesus "went into the Temple and looked

---

[1]Virgil Thompson, *Mark 13. A Study of Literary Criticism,* pp. 57-58.

around at everything," (11:11). The next day the Cleansing took place. In connection with this action Jesus makes a declaration, which we read in 11:17: that Jesus taught, and said to them, "Is it not written, 'My house shall be called a house of prayer for all nations'?" This part of Jesus' declaration is from Isaiah, and we have examined it in connection with our consideration of the Cleansing. But then Jesus goes on to add: "But you have made it a den of robbers." This second part of Jesus' declaration is drawn from Jeremiah 7. "Den of robbers" (*spelaion leiston*) appears there, and it is especially important to note that the word "abomination" (*bdelugma*) appears in the same chapter, and not just once but twice.

The Den of Robbers

The reference may be intended as a direct quotation or merely as an allusion, but it is at least clear that the statement "You have made it a "den of robbers" comes from Jer 7:11. The striking thing about "den of robbers" (*spelaion leiston*) is how inappropriate it is in its context in the Farewell Discourse. The term *leistes* does not mean "dishonest man" or "thief"; it means "robber, highwayman, bandit," or even "revolutionary, insurrectionist." If, as is often assumed, the term is intended as a characterization of the dishonest merchants and money changers who "fleeced" festival pilgrims, the quotation was not aptly chosen. The statement in John 2:16, "You shall not make my father's house a house of trade," would be much more appropriate.

It is also important to observe the way Mark uses the term *leistes* elsewhere in the Gospel. At the time of his arrest in the garden Jesus says: "Have you come out as against a robber (*leisten*) with swords and clubs, to capture me?" (14:48). The image here is not that of a dishonest merchant. And at the crucifixion the term is used to describe the two men who were crucified with Jesus (15:27). In that context the terms can only mean "revolutionary, insurrectionist." The term *leistes* is thus not an appropriate characterization for the dishonest merchants in the temple. The verse from Jeremiah has not been chosen because the image of the temple as a "den of robbers" is particularly appropriate to the historical situation involving only the merchants and money changers whom Jesus drove out of the court of the Gentiles.

Perhaps the context of Jeremiah will provide a clue to the meaning Mark has in mind. Jeremiah 7 is the famous temple sermon. The temple's presence was mistakenly interpreted as necessarily assuring God's protection. Some committed crimes and then came and stood in the temple and said, "'We are delivered,'—only to go on doing all these abominations," (vs. 10), and here the word used is *bdelugma*. And Jeremiah continues: "Has this house become a den of robbers *(spelaion leiston)* in your eyes?"

My Place at Shiloh

It is to be noted that the offenders use the temple as a place of refuge after they have committed their crimes (abominations) and that it is these abominations, committed with a sense of impunity, which turns the temple into a den of robbers. Jeremiah affirms that the Lord will not tolerate such a superstitious use of his temple. "Go to my place at Shiloh and see what I did to it for the wickedness of my people Israel." As Shiloh (eighteen miles north of Jerusalem), the earlier central shrine, was destroyed around 1050 B.C. in the days of Samuel, so also this house, desecrated by idolatry, will be destroyed. And Jeremiah returns to the same set of ideas later in the same chapter: "For the sons of Judah have done evil in my sight, says the Lord; they have set their abominations in the house which is called by my name, to defile it," (vs. 30).

In accordance with the principles and practices of *midrash*, New Testament writers often quote the Old Testament freely, using verses and passages without much regard for its original context. "But in this case, the setting of the verse in Jeremiah cannot be accidental. If the phrase 'den of robbers' is inappropriate for the historical cleansing, the verse itself is most appropriate in Mark. It is part of an oracle prophesying the destruction of the temple! The rejection of those who have misused their rights as God's chosen is in Jeremiah predicted in terms of the destruction of the temple."[2] The Den of Robbers from Jeremiah is not only historically appropriate in Mark in the Cleansing; it also fits perfectly into the context of the last chapters of his gospel. At a deeper dimension of the story the verse is important in the interpretation of the two houses, Made with Hands—Not Made with Hands (14:58). The Cleansing is important not as an isolated event, but as part of a theme that concludes with the tearing of the veil at Jesus' death (15:38). Using the Jeremiah passage, Mark characterizes the Cleansing as a prophetic anticipation of what is to come. Because they have misused the temples and their privileges, Jesus' enemies (the chief priests, elders, and scribes) have been repudiated and their temple will be destroyed. The temple Made with Hands will be replaced by a temple Not Made with Hands.

The Farewell Address ends with a forceful admonition to vigilance: "Take heed, watch; for you do not know when the time will come," (vs. 33); "Watch therefore — for you do not know when the master of the house will come," (vs. 35). Indeed, so forceful does this admonition to vigilance become that the narrator turns intrusive at the end: "And what I say to you I say to all: Watch," (vs.37).

Threefold Patterns

After the Last Supper which follows, Jesus and the disciples go out to the Mount of Olives. Jesus takes Peter, James, and John with him into Gethsemane and there he bids them: "Remain here and watch" and he goes off to pray. Then, "Jesus came and found them sleeping, and he said to Peter, 'Simon, are you asleep? Could you not watch one hour? Watch and pray that you may not enter into temptation; the spirit indeed is willing, but the flesh is weak.' And again he went away and prayed, saying the same words. And again he came and found them sleeping, for their eyes were very heavy and they did not know what to answer him. And he came the third time, and said to them, 'Are you still sleeping and taking your rest? It is enough; the hour has come; the Son of Man is betrayed into the hands of sinners," (vs. 37-41).

Gethsemane is not the only, nor the first, threefold scene in Mark's gospel. Jesus' threefold passion prediction on the way to Jerusalem we have encountered already, and two more are to follow—Peter's triple denial and the three hours of the crucifixion scene.

At Caesarea Philippi Peter's confession comes into conflict with Jesus' first passion prediction and Peter's concept of the Messiah receives correction through Jesus' suffering Son of Man. Peter's rejection of a suffering Messiah earns him the accusation of playing the role of Satan. At Caesarea Philippi the final outcome of the gospel story is already within sight. Jesus is committed to life through death—the cross is anticipated. Peter rejects the necessity of suffering—Peter's denial is anticipated.

Jesus' second prediction elicits incomprehension and fear on the part of the disciples; in effect they join the ranks of Peter. Their abandonment of Jesus is anticipated. The third prediction contrasts sharply with James' and John's request for positions of power and honor (10:35-37). By rejoinder Jesus summons them to drink the cup which he will drink. The cup is a symbol of suffering and death.

From Caesarea Philippi on, the disciples walk the way of Jesus, but they are oriented toward a goal which is different from what he had in mind. Three times Jesus pronounces in plain terms what to expect from associating with him. And three times they only hear what they want to hear.

Jesus' three visits to the disciples in the Garden both emphasize their blindness, and link up with the three passion predictions, Peter's three denials, and the three hours on the cross. Three times Jesus attempts to open the eyes of the disciples to the passion reality, but three times they remain unperceptive. Three times at Gethsemane Jesus gives his chosen disciples a chance to endorse the model of a suffering Messiah, but each time they let the occasion slip by. Three times Peter denies Jesus at the very moment the latter makes his fateful Son of Man confession. The tragic peak is reached with Jesus' three hours on the cross, the agony of which intensified from the hour of crucifixion (15:25), to the hour of demonic darkness (15:33), to the hour of abandonment, mocking and death (15:34-37). The correlation of these four threefold scenes underscores the depth of the disciples' non-understanding.

Acceptance of Suffering

In the Garden Jesus tells the chosen three: "My soul is very sorrowful, even to death," (14:34). Then, "going a little farther, he fell on the ground and prayed that, if it were possible, the hour might pass from him." Here Jesus betrays a new depth of anxiety over the prospect of suffering; he is overcome by anguish and horror in the face of death. If it were possible he would eliminate suffering from his messianic ministry. The prayer allows for the divine plan of passion. But the request for the passing of the hour and the removal of the cup has every indication of a desire to bypass the cross. The predictions had spoken of Jesus' voluntary acceptance of suffering. The lament in Gethsemane articulates Jesus' personal fear in view of death and the prayer seeks a way out of the cross. This manifests the full extent of Jesus' humanity.

The first time Jesus found his disciples asleep he said: "Watch and pray that you may not enter into temptation. The spirit indeed is willing but the flesh is weak." More is involved here than man's natural inclination to yield to physical weariness. The second time Jesus came he again found them sleeping, "for their eyes were very heavy," (14:40). This "heaviness of eyes" appears to point to a blindness on a deeper level. The disciples close their eyes to what essentially transpires at Gethsemane. Their natural sleepiness is but the outward manifestation of a nonphysical, religious blindness. Their state of fatigue signals a religious blindness which prevented them from grasping the significance of what was happening there. In the Garden Jesus came to terms with the necessity of his suffering. It is this final breakthrough toward a suffering Messiahship which the disciples slept through at Gethsemane.

On the threshold of his passion Jesus deals with the Christian's crisis of the cross. The kind of testing he undergoes at Gethsemane is the very one Christians are exposed to in the Markan setting. As they are tempted to shortcut the way to the Kingdom by avoiding the cup, so is Jesus at Gethsemane. The Jesus of Gethsemane suffers in the place of and as a model for Christians. Mark forces Jesus to the brink of recanting his passion identity because the evangelist deals with Christians who are indifferent or hostile toward a suffering Messiah.

The Naked Young Man

When Jesus was arrested the disciples "all forsook him, and fled. And a young man followed him, with nothing but a linen cloth about his body; and they seized him, but he left the linen cloth and ran away naked," (vss. 50-51). Is the young man a prefigurement of the risen Jesus, a Joseph figure, a symbol of the Christian baptismal initiate? It seems better to say, with Harry Fleddermann that the young man is simply a fleeing disciple. "The pericope is a dramatization and concretization of the universal flight of the disciples. The young man is arrested and stripped; but he flees. In contrast Jesus is arrested and stripped and crucified. The unbelieving flight of the young man is opposed to Jesus' believing acceptance of the crucifixion. Confronted with the passion the disciples all flee, even the young man. Jesus, on the other hand, fully accepts God's will. It is only after the crucifixion that care can again be bestowed on Jesus. Joseph of Arimathea buys a linen cloth and, taking Jesus' corpse down from the cross, wraps it in the linen cloth. The stripped Jesus is again covered, but only after the crucifixion."[2]

Jesus' arrest is followed by the striking Two Trial Scene, Jesus' trial before the Sanhedrin bracketed by the account of Peter's trial in the courtyard presided over by the serving girl of the high priest. In 14:54 it is reported that "Peter had followed him (Jesus) at a distance, right into the courtyard of the high priest." Once it is established that Peter is below in the courtyard the narrative returns to the scene where Jesus is being interrogated by the high priest (14:55). Following the interrogation and the rendering of the verdict against Jesus, "some began to spit on him, saying to him, 'Prophesy!'." Immediately, the narrative once again switches to Peter in the courtyard below. There Peter is questioned by the maid of the high priest. Three times he denies association with Jesus. "And immediately the cock crowed a second time. And Peter remembered how Jesus had said to him, 'Before the cock crows twice, you will deny me three times,'" (14:72).

The second time Peter was challenged "he began to invoke a curse on himself and to swear, 'I do not know this man of whom you speak,'" (vs. 71).

Peter's reaction to Jesus' first passion prediction and his denial are linked in a meaningful way. After that first prediction, "Peter took Jesus and began to rebuke him. But turning and seeing his disciples, he rebuked Peter, and said, 'Get behind me, Satan! For you are not on the side of God, but of men,'" (8:32-33). Then Jesus goes on to speak of the disciple's need to take up his cross, how he can lose his life by saving it. And Jesus concludes with the warning, "Whoever is ashamed of me and of my words, of him will the Son of Man also be ashamed," (vs. 38).

In the passion predictions Jesus corrects the messiah concept by uniting it to the Son of Man concept, and he does the same in the course of his trial. The high priest asks him if

[2]Harry Feddermann, "The Flight of a Naked Young Man (Mark 14:51-52)," *Catholic Biblical Quarterly*, 41(1979), pp. 417-18.

he is the Christ and Jesus says Yes! "And you will see the Son of Man seated at the right hand of Power," (14:62). Then we are switched out into the courtyard to witness Peter's triple denial of Jesus. After the third denial Peter "began to invoke a curse on himself and to swear, 'I do not know this man of whom you speak,'" (14:71). Debate has centered on whether this is to be understood as Peter's cursing himself (if he lies) or his cursing Jesus. But the effect is the same in either case. "Peter utters a series of curses designed to dissociate himself publicly from Jesus. The ambiguity over the object of the curse is perhaps best understood as intentional on the part of Mark who creates the highly ironic situation in which Peter either directly curses himself or indirectly does so by cursing Jesus, and by attempting to save himself in this situation in reality loses himself and is placed in even greater jeopardy. Peter, in denying Jesus, denies his own identity and becomes subject to the stern words spoken by Jesus: 'Whoever is ashamed of me and of my words, of him will the Son of Man also be ashamed,' (vs. 38)."[3]

When Jesus pronounces the first passion prediction Peter's words and actions bespeak non-understanding and opposition. In the course of his trial in the courtyard the implications are brought home to Peter (and the Christian reader). Because of his opposition Jesus had associated him with Satan. By cursing himself at his trial Peter is in grave danger of making himself fully one with Satan, until the cock's crow brings him to his senses.

---

[3]Kim E. Dewey, "Peter's Curse and Cursed Peter," in *The Passion in Mark*, ed. Werner H. Kelber (Philadelphia: Fortress, 1976), p. 101.

CHAPTER 23
THE PASSIONS OF
JOHN THE BAPTIST
AND OF JESUS

THERE IS A SPECIAL NARRATIVE PROBLEM involved in recounting the story of the just man or the prophet who is persecuted or even killed. How was it that violence had its way with him? Is this plausible? The difficulty arises from the fact that the man of God is portrayed consistently as innocent; violence must strike him without his being turned into someone guilty. The narrator must therefore find an ambiguous factor which will permit violence to strike but which will in no way detract from the innocence of the persecuted one. There are two passages in Mark where these considerations come into play: the passion of John the Baptist (6:17-29), and the passion of Jesus (Chapters 14-15). On this score alone we can anticipate that the two accounts will be similar.

In these two passion accounts the use of traditional dramatic principles and devices is especially evident: complication, reversal (*peripeteia*), and a denouement which elicits fear and pity. In the arrangement of incidents the narrator was careful to seek out (as Aristotle recommended, what is inevitable (*anagkaios*) or probable (*eikos*), "so as to make it inevitable or probable that such and such a person should say or do such and such; and inevitable or probable that one thing should follow another," (*Poetics*, XV:10). In the passion of John the Baptist[1] the first four verses (6:17-20) are the complication. Three personages are involved: Herod, John the Baptist, and Herodias. Herodias wants John dead because he has criticized her conduct, but Herod fears John. So Herodias' design is at an impasse and a reversal (*peripeteia*) is required if the action is to move forward. Just such a favorable occasion presents itself: Herod's birthday. This event is at once something special and yet probable (*eikos*), while its annual recurrence is something inevitable (*anagkaion*). The action unfolds against the background of the birthday banquet: the festive character of the occasion stands in sharp contrast to the bloody denouement which follows.

The Ambiguous Factor

A new personage is introduced, the daughter of Herodias. In the banquet context her appearance is perfectly plausible. Herod is so carried away by her dancing that he declares: "Ask me for whatever you wish, and I will grant it," (vs. 22). Without his realizing it, Herod has obligated himself to Herodias as well. The impasse is broken, and the action can proceed. The difference of points of view between Herod and Herodias is marked off in space by the entrance and the exits of the girl. She comes in to dance, goes out to consult her mother, and comes in again to make her request. The readers are in on it all; they see both sides of the scene.

The girl's request is: "I want you to give me at once the head of John the Baptist on a platter," (vs. 25). The bond which unites mother and daughter is placed at the service of the opposition which separates the mother and John the Baptist. Herod's promise and the girl's request stand in gruesome correspondence. Herod has said: "Whatever you

[1]Standaert, pp. 68-70.

ask me, I will give you, even half my kingdom," and the girl asks for John's head on a platter. By reason of the metonymy between king and kingdom, one can say that Herod is ready to cut himself in two to please the girl. Herodias does get in a blow at him, but it strikes him in the bond which unites him to the Baptist ("Herod feared John," vs. 20). It is John whose head is cut off. Afterwards the king was exceedingly sorry but he could not reverse himself "because of his oaths and his guests," (vs. 26).

The element of haste which characterizes the intervention of the girl (she reenters "immediately with haste," and asks for the head "at once") contributes to the tragic effect of the story. Likewise the fact that the girl asks for the head of John "on a platter" (vs. 25) intensifies the contrast between the banquet context and the cruelty of the crime. In the denouement (*lusis, katastrophe*) the head is passed from one to another until it ends up in the hands of the mother, who was at the origin of the tragic action.

The Just Man Condemned

Herod had John the Baptist beheaded even though he recognized him to be a "righteous and holy man," (6:20; cf. Acts 3:14). How was violence able to do its work in a plausible way and John's innocence remain unimpaired? Mark begins with a presentation of Herodias' infidelity and John the Baptist's criticism. "Thus violence gains admittance into the drama: Herodias is determined to bring John to his grave. But only a ruse will insure that violence will be able to attain its end. The ruse consists in creating a moment when the person who is an obstacle is blinded, if only for an instant. Herodias' daughter, playing the role of intermediary, accomplishes the ruse: she seduces Herod who ignores or forgets for the moment the bond which exists between mother and daughter. This moment is fatal: violence enters and, through Herod, strikes John, who is beheaded. An analogous problem is involved in recounting Jesus' death, and, in Mark, we find an identical solution."[2]

2*Ibid.*, p. 70-72.

Jesus Condemned

The passion of Jesus (Chapters 14-15) also involves a triangular relationship: the Jewish authorities, Jesus, and the crowd. The high priests and the scribes seek to put Jesus to death, but their project is at an impasse. The crowd is an obstacle, an obstacle concretized in relation to the feast of the Passover: "Not during the feast, lest there be a tumult of the people," (14:2). Ironically, as happened also in John's case, the tragic action takes place during a feast, and what is more, because of the context of the feast (release of a prisoner, 15:6).

In this case it is Judas Iscariot who brings about the first reversal. He solves the impasse blocking the high priests' strategy. The obstructing crowd can be circumvented if Jesus is arrested at night and outside the city. The narrator divides space into two zones: during the first Jesus moves about the city and temple and there he is protected by the presence of the crowd. But of an evening and at night Jesus returns to the Mount of Olives and Bethany, and there he is surrounded only by his disciples. The traitor is one who moves from the one camp to the other and makes it possible to arrest Jesus in the absence of the crowd, at night and outside the city.

The narrator is careful to point out that Judas was "one of the Twelve," (14:10). His role was therefore of the kind that Aristotle recommended in order that an action be tragic, evoking pity and fear. Those incidents seem pitiable which involve the actions of friends to each other. If an enemy does it to an enemy, there is nothing pitiable either in the deed or the intention, nor would there be if they were neither friends nor enemies. But when calamities happen among friends, "when for instance brother kills brother, or son father, or mother son, or son mother—either kills or intends to kill, or does something of the kind, that is what we must look for," (*Poetics*, XIV:9).

Judas is the friend who betrays by the sign of a kiss (14:43-45). The kiss was the conventional sign of greeting between a disciple and his master—from which comes also the vocative "Rabbi!" (14:45). By this kiss Judas points out Jesus and brings about his arrest.

When Mark related the appointment of the Twelve, he designated Judas Iscariot as the one "who betrayed him," (3:19). Beyond this Judas' action remains unexplained and unexpected. Nothing in the narrative justifies his conduct. This absence of motives for the treason can be understood as the necessary corollary of the protagonist's innocence. But, as Standaert states so well, it also involves a genuinely tragic aspect for every reader of the gospel. If Judas, one of the Twelve, could, without reason, become the one who betrayed his master, every disciple is potentially another Judas.

At the Last Supper Jesus predicts that someone would betray him, "one who is eating with me, dipping bread into the dish with me," (14:17, 20). Jesus does not name anyone; his words could be applied to anyone at the table with him. The disciples' sadness and their question ("They began to say to him one after the other, 'Is it I?,'" vs. 19) express in the narration the self-questioning that the text was designed to evoke from the readers. The dismay of the Twelve at Jesus' words cannot fail to affect these readers.

Jesus' last words concerning the traitor are: "The Son of Man goes as it is written of him, but woe to the man by whom the Son of Man is betrayed! It would be better for that man if he had not been born," (vs. 21). Here we see the "Son of Man" and "that man" set in sharp contrast. Everything that happens to the Son of Man is governed by stern necessity, because it has been willed by God; but there is also full responsibility on the part of the man who delivers up the Son of Man. This tension between responsible freedom and divine necessity is tragic in the truest sense.

"Is it I?"

The role of Judas therefore has a twofold aspect from the dramatic point of view. His interventions represent a reversal which makes it possible for the strategy of the Jewish authorities to be carried out, while his status as a disciple makes this tactical maneuver an eminently tragic action and the narrator underlines this for the readers' benefit. Peter's role in the denial scene is comparable to that of Judas. Both illustrate the seriousness of a Christian commitment. Anyone who wishes to partake in the Eucharistic meal must agree to follow Jesus in the way of suffering and even death. Judas' story shows that the possibility of turning traitor is very real. The risk is great that a Christian may flee in the time of crisis as did all the people in the gospel story, or even that he may deny Jesus as Peter did. In Peter's tears (14:72) we see the effects of the drama contained in the account.

Judas' intervention makes Jesus' arrest possible, but the drama is not yet over; only the first stage has been completed. The outcome is still awaited: how will the execution take place? Judas' role is finished and now Jesus is in the hands of the opposition, in the absence of the crowd. The judgment of the Sanhedrin only repeats the earlier condemnations, but this time more formally than ever.

Jesus is handed over to Pilate, itself the fulfillment of a prediction: "They will deliver him to the Gentiles," (10:33). But suddenly the dramatic tension reaches a new height. Although the will to do away with Jesus has triumphed up to this point, before Pilate it is threatened with frustration. Nothing up to this point has prepared for Pilate's role to decide the case. There is a real risk that the opposition's scheming will go for naught and the innocence of the accused become manifest. And, in fact, the trial before Pilate ends, at first, in a setback. Pilate's perplexity (vs. 5, "Jesus made no further answer, so that Pilate wondered") means that he has not been taken in by the strategy of the high priests and the scribes. Now everything rests in Pilate's hands and there is nothing to show that he is inclined to believe the accusations advanced by Jesus' adversaries. Indeed, Mark writes that Pilate "perceived that it was out of envy that the chief priests had delivered him up," (15:10).

Barabbas

But then comes another reversal, and the action can advance. There was a Passover custom: "At the feast the procurator used to release for them one prisoner for whom they asked," (15:6). What could be more probable (*eikos*), what more inevitable (*anagkios*), what more appropriate for a truly dramatic reversal? "The crowd came up and began to ask Pilate to do as he was wont to do for them," (vs. 8). The crowd had been circumvented by Judas' acting at night, but now we are in broad daylight, in the city, at the height of the feast. This is the critical point for the strategy of the opponents.

Pilate could only honor the custom. The crowd is sympathetic to Jesus to the point where it constitutes a serious obstacle for the realization of the high priests' design. According to all the evidence, the crowd will choose Jesus. Yet this was not to be. Barabbas makes his fateful entrance. His is a key role in the transition (*metabasis*) from the complication to the denouement.

From one point of view Jesus and Barabbas stand in sharp contrast. The one is innocent—Pilate himself indirectly bears witness to this with his question: "What evil has he done?" (15:14); the other is not only a brigand but a murderer ("Among the rebels in prison, who had committed murder in the insurrection, there was a man called Barabbas," 15:7). On the other hand, Jesus and Barabbas are alike in two respects. First, in their names. "Barabbas," "son of the father," would fit anyone. But it fitted Jesus in a unique way since from the narrative he has been in an absolute way *the son*, the one who called God "Abba" (14:36) in the same absolute way.

Then, the title "King of the Jews" is connected with both Jesus and Barabbas. As used by Pilate the title implied a rebellious attitude toward the Roman power, which is precisely why Barabbas had been thrown into prison (15:7). For its part the crowd could only wish to be liberated from the yoke of the occupying power. The sympathy of the crowd for Jesus is real even though it does not involve a perfect recognition of the mission and identity of Jesus.

When, then, Pilate addresses the crowd and asks: "Do you want me to release for you the King of the Jews?" he is maneuvering to win their favor. Jesus and Barabbas are presented as indistinguishable, and the crowd must choose. Because of this equivalence, there is no way of knowing which the crowd would choose. Pilate hopes to circumvent the high priests by having recourse to the crowd ("He perceived that it was out of envy that the chief priests had delivered him up," vs. 10). But this delivers Pilate into the hands of Jesus' enemies. The intervention of the Jewish authorities decides the question: "The chief priests stirred up the crowd to have him release for them Barabbas instead," (vs. 11).

The violent climax follows. Pilate's questions ("What shall I do with the man you call King of the Jews," vs. 12; and "What evil has he done?" vs. 14) come too late. The option has been excluded. "The double 'Crucify him' is in the logic of the option. One of the two prisoners freed, the other must suffer the penalty. Thus Barabbas as intermediary, and the momentary reduction of Jesus to the role of a leader who is contesting Roman power, overcomes the impasse in the opponents' strategy. A moment of partial blindness on Pilate's part suffices for violence to make its way and strike the innocent one. Through this ambiguous factor the three parties in balance—Pilate, the high priests, and the crowd—suddenly find themselves in agreement to condemn to death and execute a man whom the narrative presents as an innocent man."[3]

Herodias and the high priests, Herod and Pilate, the daughter of Herodias and the crowd—their roles are in full correspondence and establish a strong parallel between the two passion accounts. The occasion for the break in the impasse in the first case is Herod's birthday, in the second the feast of the Passover and the custom of liberating a

---

[3]*Ibid.*, pp. 81-82.

prisoner on this occasion. Herod's words also curiously resemble the girl's answer ("half my kingdom," "John's head"). There is the same relationship between Pilate's words and the answer of the crowd, through the intervention of Barabbas. The crowd's "Crucify him, crucify him" falls on Jesus. In both accounts everything happens contrary to expectation, nonetheless according to the greatest verisimilitude and even with implacable necessity. The tragic character of the two passions, in the sense that Aristotle understood it, stands forth clearly.

The Temple Veil

Turning now to some elements in the account of Jesus' passion, we note for one thing that Mark's account of Jesus' arraignment before the Sanhedrin is curiously convoluted. First the council "sought testimony against Jesus but they found none" (14:35). Then, "many bore false witness against him, but their witness did not agree," (vs. 56). Some of those who bore false witnes against him said: "We heard him say, 'I will destroy this temple that is made with hands, and in three days I will build another, not made with hands,'" (vs. 58).

Then once again Mark goes to the trouble of indicating the note of uncertainty. "Yet not even so did their testimony agree," (vs. 59). The testimony is ambiguous; it is apparently false, but one senses that that is not all there is to be said about it. Can it be that the testimony is also true in some sense?

Two facts provide important evidence for the meaning of the statement about the destruction of the temple in Mark's mind. First, the mention of "three days" in the charge before the Sanhedrin, and, secondly, the reference to the tearing of the temple curtain at the moment of Jesus' death (15:38). Surely the reference to "three days" is a reference to the resurrection. The result of the resurrection will be the erection of a new temple not made with hands—the Christian Church. As the "rejected stone" of Ps 118:22, mentioned in the Parable of the Vineyard, Jesus has become the "head of the corner;" as the Messiah, he is the builder of the New Temple.

But Jesus' death and resurrection also affect the old religious establishment. At the moment of his death, the "destruction" of the old order occurs. As he dies, the temple curtain is torn from top to bottom. Clearly, for Mark, the event is the fulfillment of the "prophecy" made in the charge, and repeated in the taunts at the cross: "You who would destroy the temple: save yourself," (15:29). With Jesus' death, the old religious order comes to an end; those who have rejected Jesus, the religious leaders, have now been rejected by God. Jesus is the destroyer of the temple in a figurative and in an ironic sense: its destruction is a result of his death, brought about by those in charge of the temple worship. This suggests that the charge before the Sanhedrin can be both "false testimony" (Jesus never threatened to destroy the temple) and "prophetic" (as a result of his death the old religious establishment symbolized by the temple comes to an end).

The tearing of the temple veil is a second clue to Mark's understanding of the charge before the Sanhedrin. The tearing of the veil represents a culmination of the temple theme: "In a supernatural fashion the temple itself sets the scoffers at naught by bearing witness to the doom to which it is condemned."[4]

The presence of the verse immediately following Jesus' death suggests that with Jesus' death, the temple establishment comes to an end—or at least a decisive sign is given that its doom is sealed. One result of Jesus' death is the end of the temple order. This represents a partial fulfillment of the "prophecy" made at the trial; Mark views the charge as true in some sense. At the moment of death Jesus uttered a loud cry and then breathed his last. Then Mark adds: "And the curtain of the temple was torn in two, from top to

---

[4]T. A. Burkill, *Mysterious Revelation*, (Ithaca: Cornell University Press, 1963), p. 138.

bottom," (15:38). Thus, with Jesus' death, the negative half of the prediction is fulfilled. The corresponding fulfillment of the prediction of a new "temple not made with hands" after three days is also fulfilled.

Speculation about Elijah as the eschatological prophet was present in the minds of those who witnessed or wrote about the events described in the New Testament. This is also true of Mark, as was made evident to us from the role that John the Baptist plays in the Prologue. As we saw earlier, D. Daube has pointed out that such speculation may account for two incidents not so far associated with Elijah: the way in which Jesus is acclaimed on entering Jerusalem (see Chapter 19), and the rending of the veil of the temple.

Rent in Two Parts

Mark tells us that, on Jesus' death, "the veil of the temple was rent in twain from the top to the bottom." Codex Bezae and the Itala are even more explicit: "it was rent in two parts," not just "in twain."

First we should take note of what Elisha did and said when his master, Elijah, ascended into heaven. "Elisha saw it and he cried, 'My father, my father!' the chariots of Israel and its horsemen!'. . . And he took hold of his clothes and rent them in two pieces," (2 Kings 2:12). In rabbinic times, there were prescribed occasions on which a man had to rend his garment. Furthermore, taking note of the phrase "in two pieces" in our text, they prescribed that in certain cases, the two parts into which you have rent your garment may never be sewn together again. These cases include the death of your father, your mother, your teacher of Torah; the receipt of terrible news; the utterance of a blasphemy by someone in your presence; and, finally, the destruction of Judaean cities, the temple, or Jerusalem.

"When we consider the stress laid in the New Testament on the complete splitting of the curtain into two—or, according to some readings, two parts—from top to bottom, it is safe to find here an allusion to the rite practised as a sign of deepest sorrow. We need not decide whether the death of Jesus is likened to that of a teacher of Torah or to the destruction of the temple. Either or both comparisons may play some part, as also the idea that those responsible for the crucifixion are the real blasphemers, and not Jesus at whose words the High Priest had rent his clothes."[5]

The precise way in which Mark represents the tearing of the veil seems to connect the event with a mourning rite—and, indeed, with the prototype, in rabbinic eyes, of this rite, the action of Elisha on Elijah's ascension. We should also take note of a possible connection between the incident of the veil and Jesus' Ascension. In Elijah's assumption we read that the chariot of fire "separated the two of them and Elijah went up into heaven." In his description of Jesus' ascension Luke writes that Jesus "parted from them and was carried up into heaven," (24:51). The incident of the veil may be another of Mark's foreshadowings, this time of the Ascension.

The tearing of the veil may also be viewed as a sign of mourning for the approaching end of the temple. The word *pargodh*, which in the Targum stands for the curtain separating the holy of holies from the outer chamber, may also denote a tunic. The extension of the custom of rending one's garment to the veil of the temple—the tunic of the temple—would have been a natural one. Finally, as Jesus cries out, "*Eloi, Eloi, lama sabachthani,*" some bystanders think he is summoning Elijah and mockingly remark, "Wait, let us see whether Elijah will come to take him down." "After this, the rending in two of the veil of the temple, reminiscent as it is of what Elisha did when his master was translated, may well be intended as an answer to the mockery: here is Elijah himself, or one that is greater."[6]

[5]Daube, p. 24.

[6]Daube, p. 25.

CHAPTER 24
CLOSURE

AND THE WOMEN "WENT OUT AND FLED from the tomb; for trembling and astonishment had come upon them; and they said nothing to any one, for they were afraid," (Mark 16:8).

At an early date there were Christians who felt that this was not a suitable closure for a gospel. They were probably influenced by the other gospels, all of which have resurrection appearances. They may also have felt that Mark's closure did not fulfill expectations raised in the gospel, which a proper closure is supposed to do. Acting on these convictions they added closures of their own — the longer ending(s).

The literary concept "closure" refers to a sense of literary ending derived from the satisfaction of textually generated expectations. It should give a sense that the narrative has terminated and that in terminating it has reached its goal. The closure is both the point towards which the narrator has been working and the point from which his narrative can be construed.

In Mark's closure it does seem for a moment that one expectation at least is to be fulfilled. The disciples are to be told that Jesus is going before them to Galilee where they will see him (16:7) as he had predicted (14:28). But the fulfillment is short-circuited by 16:8, for the women "said nothing to anyone." Then the text ends. But the reader's work is just beginning. The short-circuited expectation "requires the reader to review what he has read in order to comprehend this apparent incongruity and its meaning for the narrator's message."[1] If this is the case, 16:8 is a very effective closure indeed.

In our survey of Mark's narrative we have, for one thing, seen a regular pattern of predictions and fulfillments. What Jesus intends and predicts comes to pass despite the intent and action of other characters in the story, whether his enemies or his all too fallible disciples. Jesus' prediction about meeting his disciples in Galilee was made with full foreknowledge of the Twelve's imminent defection. Nonetheless the young man declares that Jesus' intention is to be realized. This intention can no more be frustrated by the women's disobedience than it could be by the disciples' defection. Even while they are muddling about, as the disciples and the establishment had previously muddled about, Jesus, having risen, is on his way to Galilee where the disciples will soon see him.

Mark's closure is also an artful bridge between the discourse and story levels. The plotted narrative (discourse) comes to an end with a reference to an event that will happen subsequently on the story level (the meeting in Galilee). The women's disobedience (in both its positive and negative aspects) strikes a note of continuity between the two levels. At the same time we are carried back to the time when Jesus predicted that event (14:28), and this prediction is intimately connected with those other predictions Jesus made in his Farewell Discourse (Chapter 13). And this affords us an opportunity to reflect on the discontinuity between Mark's description of the apostles of Jesus' time and Jesus' description of the apostles of the implied reader's time, as contained especially in the Farewell Address.

---

[1]Norman R. Petersen, "When is the End not the End? Literary Reflections on the Ending of Mark's Narrative," *Interpretation*, 34(1980), 153.

In Mark's story prior to Galilee the disciples did not understand what Jesus said about the relationship between the Son of Man, Messiah, and Kingdom, whereas in Jesus' story the disciples (in their principal representatives) uphold Jesus' position and do so in opposition to others (false messiahs and their prophets) who now hold their former mistaken views.

Implied Reader

A number of literary concepts have stood us in good stead in our analysis of Mark's gospel: narrative (especially in its dramatic form), story and discourse, and closure. For our summation the concept of implied author and implied reader may prove most useful.

In his recent book on literary theory Seymour Chatman writes: "A narrative is a communication; hence, it presupposes two parties, a sender and a receiver. Each party entails three different personages. On the sending end are the real author, the implied author, and the narrator (if any); on the receiving end, the real audience (listener, reader, viewer), the implied audience, and the narratee."[2] The implied author is implied because he must be reconstructed by the reader from the narrative. He has no direct voice; he instructs us through the design of the whole narrative. The implied author is seen most clearly by comparing different narratives written by the same real author but presupposing different implied authors with different personalities. An unreliable narrator is at odds with the implied author.

The implied reader, the counterpart of the implied author, is the audience presupposed by the narrative itself. Wayne Booth calls him the "postulated reader," pointing out that from the author's viewpoint, a successful reading of his book must eliminate all distance between the essential norms of his implied author and the norms of the postulated

---

[2]*Story and Discourse*, Narrative Structure in Fiction and Film, (Ithaca: Cornell University Press, 1978), p. 28.

reader. "An author finds that some of the beliefs on which a full appreciation of his work depends come ready-made, fully accepted by the postulated reader as he comes to the book, and some must be implanted or reinforced."[3] Our survey of Mark's gospel leaves little doubt about what truths those are for the implied author of Mark.

Beliefs Reinforced

The implied writer of Mark is a Christian who narrates the public life of Jesus, with concentration on the experience of the disciples responding to Jesus' call, and shapes his narrative to be of maximum benefit to his Christian readers. Let the disciples' experience serve to correct the readers' mistakes! We can see what those mistakes are by taking note of those things toward which Mark has a negative attitude. These include: family (nepotism?), discipleship without sacrifice, ambition, son of David messianism, Jerusalem, and an expectation of the continued presence of the Risen Jesus. Nonetheless, for the implied author those disciples truly hold the positions assigned to them. And in the course of the narrative several signals are given that their non-understanding would be dispelled and that Jesus would reestablish contact with them.

The implied reader, the counterpart of the implied author, is the audience presupposed by the narrative itself. This implied reader is already a Christian but whose view of the Church is unrealistic. As the disciples had felt that Jesus' messiahship had not sufficiently satisfied their temporal, political expectations, so the implied readers wish that the Church they knew was more satisfying in these respects. Often they are as ambitious for positions of power and honor as the sons of Zebedee, and family considerations are often involved. Often they are as lacking in vigilance as the disciples in Gethsemane. Some find it difficult to face up to the indications Jesus had given that contact with Jerusalem

---

[3] *The Rhetoric of Fiction*, (Chicago: University of Chicago Press, 1961), p. 177.

and its temple would be denied them. They had not accepted the fact that they could not rely on the continued, sensible intervention of the Risen Lord on their behalf—that their pilgrim existence would be characterized as much by the absence of the Lord as by his presence.

For a time the disciples conform to the truth and goodness with which Jesus is identified, and the reader can identify with them during this phase. But then the disciples' behavior comes to be characterized by incomprehension, and a tension is set up, a tension internal to the narrative between Jesus and the disciples. But this tension raises in the readers' mind the possibility of another tension, an external tension, between his own behavior and Jesus' truth and goodness. After identifying with the disciples early in the gospel, the negative turn in the disciples' story leads the reader to reexamine his own discipleship.

The purpose of the author of Mark was not merely to present certain ideas about Jesus but to lead his readers through a particular story in which they could discover themselves and thereby change. The tension between Jesus and the disciples, internal to the story, mirrors an external tension between the Church as the author perceives it and the discipleship to which it is called.

Perhaps we can sum the whole thing up by saying that Mark wanted to exclude a *theologia gloriae*.[4] Since he alludes to resurrection appearances, Mark knew of them but chose not to describe any. It was his purpose to place Christology so solidly within the context of the Passion that it would be impossible to separate resurrection from suffering.

The reader of Mark is confronted with the idea of a resurrection (as a promise) from 8:31 on, but, significantly, 8:31 is the first of the passion predictions. At the points where epiphany is strongest and the theology of glory most possible, Mark applies the counterweight of the messianic

---

[4]Cf. Andreas Lindemann, "Die Osterbotschaft des Markus. Zur theologischen Interpretation von Mark 16. 1-8," *New Testament Studies* 26(3, 1980), 298-317.

secret. As Jesus and the disciples came down from the mountain of the Transfiguration, Jesus "charged them to tell no one what they had seen," (9:9). It is solidly within the context of the Passion that Jesus gives an answer to the question: "Are you the Christ?"

Proclamation to Both Women and Reader

The "young man's" word to the women, "He is risen!" is the only reference in Mark to Jesus' resurrection as a historical happening. And the women are to go and tell the disciples that Jesus is going before them to Galilee. In this way the gaze of the disciples (and of the reader) is drawn away from the empty tomb. But the women remain silent. So it also transpires that both 'the women and later Christians hear the resurrection proclamation on the same basis. The resurrection proclamation is spoken directly to both women and reader.

By his messianic secret Mark limits the traditional references to Jesus' messiahship and arranges that these references be seen only in the context of cross and suffering. So miracles are often followed by a command to silence. The stronger epiphany and revelation appeared in Mark's source, the heavier the counterweight in Mark's presentation. And since epiphany is stronger in the resurrection than in any pre-Easter miracle, it was inevitable that Mark should use some device at that point in his story such as his very adroit 16:1-8.

Mark establishes his defense against a theology of glory in two stages. First, he breaks off the messianic secret not on Easter Sunday but on Good Friday. The Roman centurion acknowledges Jesus at the foot of the Cross: "Truly this man was the Son of God!" (15:39). Yet, in a sense, the messianic secret is not broken off but is continued through the lack of resurrection appearances. The messianic secret could not be used in the midst of a resurrection appearance, so Mark substituted the silence of the women and the lack of resurrection appearances.